DYNAMIC MODERN WOMEN

ATHLETES

Laurie Lindop

Twenty-First Century Books
A Division of Henry Holt and Company
New York

*For my coach, Barbara Welsh, and
my teammate, Tracey Lavery.*

⤳

Twenty-First Century Books
A Division of Henry Holt and Company, Inc.
115 West 18th Street
New York, NY 10011

Henry Holt® and colophon are trademarks of
Henry Holt and Company, Inc.
Publishers since 1866

Text copyright © 1996 by Laurie Lindop
All rights reserved.
Published in Canada by Fitzhenry & Whiteside Ltd.
195 Allstate Parkway, Markham, Ontario L3R 4T8

Library of Congress Cataloging-in-Publication Data
Lindop, Laurie.
Athletes / Laurie Lindop.—1st ed.
p.   cm.—(Dynamic modern women)
Includes bibliographical references and index.
Summary: Highlights the lives and athletic accomplishments of
ten women: Lynette Woodard, Diana Nyad, Kristi Yamaguchi,
Florence Griffith Joyner, Julie Krone, Monica Seles, Nancy Lopez,
Bonnie Blair, Kim Zmeskal, and Joan Benoit Samuelson.
1. Women athletes—Biography—Juvenile literature. [1. Athletes.
2. Women—Biography.] I. Title. II. Series.
GV697.A1L566   1996
796.092'2-dc20
[B]   96-11429
                                                                        CIP
                                                                         AC

ISBN 0-8050-4167-2
First Edition—1996

Designed by Kelly Soong

Printed in Mexico
All first editions are printed on acid-free paper.∞
1 3 5 7 9 10 8 6 4 2

Photo credits

pp. 6, 16, 26, 36, 46, 56, 66, 78, 102: Focus on Sports; p. 90: Patinage Artistique/
Gamma Liaison.

CONTENTS

INTRODUCTION

These are the stories of contemporary women athletes who are among today's record holders, Olympic champions, and national heroes. Their stories tell about sacrifice and unswerving dedication. These women have pushed their bodies to the limits of endurance. They have battled back from injuries and bouts of self-doubt. They have all spent long hours practicing, training, conditioning.

Not so long ago, their accomplishments would have seemed unimaginable because many sports were seen as appropriate only for men and boys. The women in this book have swum through shark-infested waters and bench-pressed two hundred pounds. They have set world records in speed skating and the 100-meter dash. They have trailblazed their way into the formerly all-male domains of horse racing and professional basketball. Many have had to battle sexual discrimination; others have refused to be beaten by racism or poverty. All have dazzled fans with their agility, grace, speed, and strength. They are the women for whom second best was never good enough. They are all champions.

ONE

❦

BONNIE BLAIR

Nicknamed "America's kid sister," speed skater Bonnie Blair has an engaging, bubbly personality when she's off the ice. However, as soon as she put on her skates, an iron-willed competitive spirit would come to the fore. "There's a certain something that happens when that gun goes off," she said. "I'm almost two totally different people. . . . It's that mind-set or that tunnel vision. I'm not going to let anything get in the way of how I compete."[1]

Bonnie Blair skated to win, to set world records, to go faster than any woman had ever gone before, sometimes in excess of thirty-five miles per hour! She was the most successful American female Olympic athlete in history, winning five gold medals and a bronze. Her success helped focus a spotlight on the relatively unknown sport of speed skating.

Olympic speed skaters compete on an oval rink the same size as most running tracks—400 meters around. Two competitors race at the same time, but instead of racing against each other, they race against the clock. To be as aerodynamic as possible, they lean forward, bending at the waist, swinging their arms for added power. The skater who finishes in the fastest time overall is the winner. Sometimes there is only a tenth or even a hundredth of a second separating the winner from the second-place finisher. To be a champion, a skater must have tremendous leg strength, speed, and flawless technique. Bonnie Blair had all three.

She said, "It's an amazing sport. It's the fastest that humans can go [under their own power] without the help of gravity. . . . You ultimately realize that you're always competing against yourself. It's just you and whatever you bring to the starting line on that particular day."[2]

The youngest of six children, Bonnie Blair was born on March 18, 1964, in Cornwall, New York. Both of Bonnie's parents, Charlie and Eleanor Blair, loved skating and took their children out onto the ice almost as soon as they could walk. When Bonnie was two years old, the family moved to Champaign, Illinois, because her father had been offered a job as a sales manager for a concrete company. She recalled that she learned how to skate shortly after arriving in Illinois. "If I wanted to be with my brothers and sisters," she said, "I had to go to the [ice] track. They didn't have skates to fit me at that time, so they left my shoes on inside the skates."[3]

By the time Bonnie was four years old, she was competing in skating races at the local hockey rink. In these races four or more children would race at the same time. Bonnie discovered it was important to get off to a fast start or else she would be trapped behind the other skaters. There was nothing she loved better than the feel of breaking free from the pack and gliding across the finish line in first place.

By the time she entered Centennial High School, other activities also began to appeal to her. She joined the cheerleading squad, gymnastics and track teams, and was elected to the student council. At this time, Cathy Priestner, a Canadian speed skater and Olympic silver medalist, saw Bonnie skate. She told Bonnie that if she worked hard, she would be good enough to make it to the Olympics.

"Cathy was around at exactly the right time in my life," Bonnie said. "She got me to work on my skating all year round instead of just during the winter months."[4] With Cathy's help, fifteen-year-old Bonnie was soon skating fast enough to qualify for the 1980 Olympic trials. The winners at the trials would qualify for the U.S. Olympic team. Although Bonnie narrowly missed making the team, she realized that with more work, she could be good enough to compete at the 1984 Olympics.

There was one problem, however. The track in her hometown was only 110 meters long. An Olympic track was almost four times that size. Bonnie knew that she needed to practice on a larger track. The closest one was in Milwaukee, and her father could not afford to send her to train away from home.

Bonnie refused to give up and recalled that there was a Cops for Kids program in her town that made money available for special causes. Maybe, she thought, this would include financial aid for a young skater.

In 1981 she spoke with the policemen in charge. One of them recalled, "We had no idea what speed-skating was, but we told her, 'You skate, we'll raise the money.'"[5] They held bake sales and car washes and sold candy bars to raise $7,500 for Bonnie, enough to pay for her to begin training in Milwaukee.

The experience of skating on a long track paid off, and Bonnie Blair earned a spot on the 1984 U.S. Olympic team. She was thrilled to have the opportunity to compete in the games held in Sarajevo, which at that time was the capital of Yugoslavia. She recalled, "I was in awe the whole time. I mean I'd sit in the dining hall with [famous figure skater] Scott Hamilton. . . . My mouth would be on the ground. I'd sit. . . saying, 'Hey, I'm here with them. This is just amazing.'"[6]

On the day of the 500-meter speed-skating event, Bonnie finished in eighth place. She was pleased with her performance but wanted to do better at the next Olympics. "People look only at the medals," Bonnie said. "We were right there. The times are so close. One little slip can cost you a medal."[7]

After the Olympics, Bonnie moved to Butte, Montana, to work with U.S. speed-skating coach Mike Crowe. Until then she admitted that she had been "lazy about training. If I had something else I wanted to do, I did it." But in Montana that all changed. Now, she said, "If I missed a workout, I felt guilty about it and made it up."[8] To build strength, she lifted weights. To improve her aerobic capacity, she jogged and biked. To increase her speed, she would ice-skate in winter and roller-skate in summer.

Her coach recognized that Bonnie was going to be a world-class skater. "Where the others tend to run a bit more [off the starting line]," he said, "Bonnie gets into her skating stroke right away. She reaches full stride faster than anyone."[9] Bonnie attributed these quick starts to her early years as a pack skater when she had to learn to get out fast, or not at all.

By 1986 Bonnie was the world champion in short-track skating and was anxious to compete in meets in Europe. With help from the Champaign police officers, she gathered enough money to race in countries all over Europe. In the Netherlands she set a world record for the 500 meters and inspired enthusiastic fans to start singing a heavily accented version of "My Bonnie Lies Over the Ocean."

Soon the media was picking Bonnie to win the 500-meter race at the 1988 Olympics in Calgary, Canada. They also considered her a contender in the 1000- and 1500-meter events.

Nineteen members of her family came to Calgary to cheer her on, but Bonnie didn't spend much time with them. She knew she needed to focus on her skating. This was hard since the Olympic village was buzzing with excitement. Bonnie spent as much time as possible alone in her room, watching the events on television. Over and over again she envisioned the race. The tiniest mistake, she knew, would make the difference between winning and losing. But Bonnie relied on her hours of training and preparation. She knew she could not worry about how fast her competitors skated. "I just had to worry about myself," she said, "and what I have to do."[10]

On the day of the race, Bonnie pulled on her red, white, and blue skintight outfit, and tightly laced her skates. She could see the signs cheering her on that her family had hung on the walls of the stadium.

The speed-skating event was being held in an indoor arena, and without wind the races would be especially fast. Bonnie knew her main competition would come from East German skater Christa Rothenburger, who had won a gold medal in 1984 and who would skate in two heats ahead of her. Bonnie watched her glide up to the starting line. She looked strong and confident. When the starter's gun sounded, Christa raced off to a world record, finishing in 39.12 seconds. She'd thrown down her glove—the challenge was on.

Bonnie felt ready. She dug the toe of her blade into the ice, squatted in ready position. At the gun, she raced to a fast start, her hands slicing the air, her blades gliding over the hard, glistening ice. As she passed the 100-meter mark, the announcer called out her time—10.55 seconds, 0.02 second faster than Rothenburger's time. Bonnie tore down the backstretch of ice, and as she crossed the finish line she looked up at the clock and saw that she had set a new world record—39.10 seconds! She had won the gold medal!

Standing on the champion's platform listening to the national anthem, she tried to fight back the tears but could not. In the stands, her family were also teary eyed.

Bonnie went on to win a bronze in the 1000 meters and placed fourth in the 1500 meters. She became the only American multiple medal winner at the games, and her teammates voted to give her the honor of carrying the American flag in the closing ceremonies. When she returned home, she was invited to the White House with the rest of the Olympic team.

Shaking President Ronald Reagan's hand, the girl from Champaign realized she had come a long way.

By 1990 Bonnie had won five consecutive U.S. sprint championships, and one fellow skater said, "Bonnie doesn't have any competition in this country."[11] Without anyone to challenge her, she found it hard to keep her competitive edge and began to search for ways to sustain her level of fitness and speed. She decided to start cycling and moved to Indianapolis to train. She finished fourth in her first national sprint competition and made the United States Women's Cycling team. Then she began to worry about what would happen if she fell and decided to quit cycling and return to skating.

The 1990-1991 season was a difficult one for Bonnie. During the winter, she contracted bronchitis (a lung infection), which made breathing difficult and sapped her energy. Also, the Persian Gulf War was raging, and the U. S. government was afraid that American athletes in Europe might become targets of terrorist attacks. So Bonnie would race in Europe, then fly back to America. So much traveling was exhausting. At the world sprint-speed-skating championships, she placed a disappointing fifth overall. She said, "[It] was so frustrating. I'd look down at my feet and feel I had someone else's skates on."[12]

She started training with a new coach and found the change helped revitalize her workouts as well as her skating. She would wake at dawn, eat, stretch, work out, eat, nap, stretch, work out, eat, and fall asleep. Climbing into bed at night, Bonnie said, was "my favorite part of the day. I mean I just collapsed. Woomph."[13] At the Olympic trials in Milwaukee Bonnie easily outraced all of her competition.

The 1992 Olympics were being held in Albertville, France. This time almost fifty relatives arrived at the skating arena in a double-decker bus, waving American flags out the window. Many donned purple-and-white windbreakers designed by

Bonnie's brother, Rob. The media called them the "Blair Bunch." On the day of the 500-meter race, they led the audience in a rousing chorus of "My Bonnie Lies Over the Ocean!"

At the starting line, Bonnie said, "I knew they were there . . . . But they were just a blur, and I couldn't identify anyone. I wasn't just giving it my best for myself. I was also thinking of my father [who had died in 1989]. He knew I would go to the Olympics before I knew I would. I always thought my father was crazy, but somehow he knew I'd get here."[14]

When the gun went off, Bonnie's strong, perfect strides sent her whizzing over the ice. At the 100-meter mark she posted the fastest time of the day, and after that, she picked up her pace. As she crossed the finish line in first place, she became the first American woman to win back-to-back gold medals in the 500 meters. Afterward she said, "We're just beginning."[15] She still had the 1500- and 1000-meter races to go.

In the 1500 meters it was soon clear that she was too far off the pace to win, and her coach signaled her to slow down and conserve energy for the 1000-meter race later in the week. Bonnie won the 1000 meters, setting a track record and beating the second-place finisher by only 0.02 second! "It's not very much," Bonnie said, "but it's enough to win. So I'll take it!"[16]

After Albertville, people began speculating that Bonnie might decide to retire. But a quirk in the Olympic schedule meant that the next winter Olympics would be held two years later, in 1994 rather than in 1996. Bonnie promised her fans that she would go for the gold again.

She began training with a new coach, Nick Thometz, at a new indoor skating rink in Milwaukee. "We changed things quite a bit," Bonnie said. "Our emphasis was more on the quality of the work, not the quantity."[17] This strategy paid off. During the 1993-94 season, Bonnie lost only one 500-meter race and captured the 1994 overall gold medal at the world sprint skating championships. Going into the Olympics in Lillehammer, Norway, Coach Thometz said, "I've never seen a competitor as mentally tough as Bonnie. To perform the way she has in pressure situations time after time, takes a remarkable ability to focus and forget distractions."[18]

At the Olympic Village, Bonnie knew she would need to focus on her skating and try to ignore all the media hype that was making her the skater to beat. This time sixty Blair Bunch family members went to Norway. Wearing shiny gold baseball caps that read "Go Bonnie Gold!" they received almost as much media attention as the Olympic champ. "Sometimes I think [my mother] was on TV more than I was!" Bonnie laughed. [19]

But when it came time for the 500-meter race, all cameras were turned on Bonnie. The huge stadium grew hushed as she waited at the starting line. When the gun went off, the other skaters watched her wide-eyed; her technique was flawless. At the 100-meter mark it was clear she was skating the fastest she had all year. She crossed the finish line in 39.25 seconds. This time put her in first place, but other good skaters were waiting for their chance to take away the gold. One after another they tried, but none could beat Bonnie's time. She had won her third consecutive gold medal in the 500 meters! The Blair Bunch was ecstatic. Still wearing her skates, Bonnie clambered into the stands to celebrate with them.

As the press engulfed her, Bonnie said, "That was a big race for me and I'm really happy for that. A little faster would have been nice, but I'm happy with it."[20] Then she set her sights on her next race, the 1500 meters. She put in a personal best for the long race, but it was only good enough for third place. Later she was bumped down to fourth.

There was only one race left—the 1000 meters—in Bonnie's Olympic career. After racing off to a quick start, she faltered about halfway through, putting her hand down on the ice. "Oh no!" the Blair Bunch gasped. But Bonnie recovered and skated flawlessly to the end. No other skater would come close to her that afternoon. In fact, she won by the largest ever margin in a women's Olympic 1000 meter event—the gap between Blair and the second-place finisher was larger than that between the second-place finisher and the six-teenth!

Bonnie Blair had won five gold medals, more than any fe-male Olympic athlete in history. That evening, long after the lights went out in the stadium and the stands had emptied, she continued skating around and around on the darkened ice, saying good-bye to her Olympic career.

After Lillehammer, her life was hectic. She traveled across the country, giving motivational speeches and appearing on the *Today* show and CBS *This Morning*. She filmed commercials and attended many other publicity events.

Many fans assumed she would retire after Lillehammer, but Bonnie had one more goal. She wanted not only to beat her own 500-meter world record time of 39.10 seconds but also to shatter the 39-second mark. "This was like the ulti-mate barrier of the four-minute mile for track," she explained.

At the World Championships in Calgary in March 1994, Bonnie crossed the finish line in 38.99 seconds. "I'll never for-get seeing those numbers," she said. "Who would have thought that, at the age of 30, I would have been able to go faster than I ever had?"[21]

After that feat, Bonnie knew she was ready to retire. She decided that the perfect closing event would be the 1995 World Championships, which were being held at the rink where she practiced in Milwaukee. "I'd like to finish up on my own turf," she said.[22] On the day of the World Championships, three hundred raucous Blair Bunch members came to cheer her on. In the 500 meters, she skated across the finish line in first place—a fitting end to a remarkable career.

After retiring she said that she might go to college or do some coaching. But one thing was certain—she would stay involved with the sport she loved so much. "I want to give something back," Bonnie declared.[23]

TWO

FLORENCE GRIFFITH JOYNER

When sprinter Florence Griffith Joyner showed up at the starting line at the 1988 Olympic trials in a brightly colored, one-legged running suit, she knew that everyone's eyes would be focused on her. And that's exactly what she wanted. That afternoon, "Flo-Jo" shattered the 100-meter dash world record.

"Don't let anyone tell you what you can't do," she said later. "Don't listen to the can'ts. Believe in yourself, and things will happen."[1]

Delorez Florence Griffith was born on December 21, 1959, the seventh child in a family of eleven. They lived in the Mojave Desert of California. When Florence was four, her mother left her husband and moved with her children into a housing project in the poor Watts neighborhood of Los Angeles.

"We had nothing," her mother recalled.[2] But she was committed to helping her children succeed and was a strict disciplinarian. During the week, the children were not permitted to watch television and everyone had to be in bed by ten P.M.

On Wednesdays they had "powwows" when they would use the Bible to discuss what they had done wrong. Florence's older sister recalled, "Mama would have to holler, 'Lock the doors, it's powwow time. Otherwise Florence was gone."[3]

Always independent minded, Florence never liked to follow the crowd. She said, "I'd wear one green sock and one blue sock. One rolled up, one down. Braid my hair at the top, sticking straight up."[4] If her friends at school laughed at her, she'd just laugh along with them.

Even her choice in pets was unusual—a boa constrictor. "I bathed her and lotioned her," Florence said. "When she shed, I saved all of her skin and painted it different colors."[5]

Florence's creativity was not the only thing that made her stand out; she was also a phenomenal natural athlete. Her mother said, "She was so light on her feet. She just floated."[6] When she ran, no one could keep up with her. On visits to her father's house in the desert, she would spend hours chasing jackrabbits. When she was seven years old, Florence won her first sprinting competition at a local track meet.

At Jordan High School Florence was a good student. She also became a track star, setting school records in sprints and the long jump. At this time, she met another Watts girl, Valerie Brisco, who would become her longtime rival.

After graduating Florence decided to attend California State University (Cal State) at Northridge because the school had a talented track coach named Bobby Kersee. After her freshmen year, Florence could not afford to return to school and had to take a job as a bank teller. Coach Kersee refused to let his talented sprinter leave and helped her get financial aid.

Shortly after Florence returned to school, Kersee took an assistant's coaching job at the University of California at Los Angeles (UCLA)—a school with a top-notch reputation in track and field. Suddenly Florence had to make a difficult decision: Would she follow Kersee or stay at Cal State? She said, "I had a 3.25 GPA in business, [and] UCLA didn't even offer my major. . . . But my running was starting up, and I knew that Bobby was the best coach for me. "[7] She enrolled at UCLA and began training seriously. She also started growing her fingernails and painting them rainbow colors. At one point, her curved talons reached six and a half inches in length!

By 1980 Coach Kersee felt Florence was good enough to compete in the 200-meter (halfway around the track) sprint event at the Olympic trials. If she placed in the top three, she would win a place on the United States team and would compete at the games being held in Moscow.

Although she ran hard, Florence finished fourth. Adding to her disappointment was the fact that her rival, Valerie Brisco, made the Olympic team. As it turned out, the team did not compete because the United States boycotted the Olympics to protest the Soviet Union's invasion of Afghanistan.

Florence's narrow loss at the trials spurred her to work even harder. By 1982 she was the National Collegiate Athletic Association (NCAA) champion in the 200 meters.

In 1984 she once again competed in the Olympic trials and this time won a spot on the 200-meter team. She was invited to join the relay team also, but only if she cut her long nails so she would not stab her teammate when passing the baton. Florence refused and was not allowed on the team.

Still, Florence looked forward to competing in the 200 meters and was especially excited that the 1984 Olympics were being held in Los Angeles. She was disappointed, however, to find out that the Soviet Union, East Germany, and other countries would not compete in response to the U.S. boycott at the previous Olympics. Some of the best runners in the world would not be racing at the Olympics.

On the day of the 200-meter race, Florence crouched down in the starting blocks. She had painted her nails red, white, and blue. One nail was painted gold—symbolizing her hope for a first-place finish. When the gun went off, Florence blazed down the track and crossed the finish line in second place, behind her rival, Valerie Brisco. Florence was disappointed. Not only had she lost to Brisco; she felt she might not even have won any medal if the runners from the Communist bloc countries had been competing.

Discouraged, Florence quit training, gained about fifteen pounds, and took a job in a bank. She also began braiding hair for friends and relatives. In her free time, she dated Al Joyner, the 1984 Olympic triple-jump champion. "He's so positive," Florence said. "He's the guy I dreamed about."[8] On October 10, 1987, they were married in Las Vegas.

Al urged Florence to start training again. He thought that if she worked hard she could win a gold at the 1988 Olympics. Florence began training with Al and Coach Kersee, and by the time she entered the 1987 World Championships in Rome, she had lost weight and felt she was back in tip-top shape. She even figured she had a good chance of coming in first in the 200 meters. But once again she came in second.

She said, "I'd *always* come in second. . . . When you've been second best for so long, you can either accept it, or try to become the best. [After Rome] I made the decision to try and be the best in [the Olympics of] 1988."[9]

With gritty determination, Florence trained harder than ever before. "If you want to run [as fast as] a man, you have to train like a man," she said, "and weights are the main factor."[10] Weight lifting helped her build up the muscles in her upper thighs. Eventually, she was so strong she could do squats with 320 pounds on her shoulders!

Florence took an employee relations job at a company that allowed her to work only four hours a day as part of its "Jobs for Olympians" program. Afternoons she would go to the track for a workout, then to the weight room. After dinner she would have another late-night workout, sometimes sprinting around the track long after midnight. "There were times when I wouldn't sleep for forty-eight hours because of everything I had to do," she said.[11]

A few days before the Olympic trials, Florence and Al went for one of their training runs, racing each other to the corner of their street. That evening, as they sprinted down the sidewalk, Al whispered to her, "Don't tense up, stay relaxed."[12] Suddenly Florence whizzed ahead of him. "It was like afterburners ignited on her feet," he recalled.[13] That evening Florence learned the secret of all great runners—to run faster by trying less hard. Staying relaxed allowed her muscles to move together more fluidly, increasing her speed.

Going into the trials, the media paid little attention to Florence. But this didn't bother her. She was looking forward to startling everyone with her newfound speed—and with the fourteen wild outfits she planned to wear at the trials. She had discovered the style by accident. "I was trying for a new idea," she said, "and had cut one leg off some tights, and happened to look in the mirror and said, 'That might work.'"[14] These outfits in dazzling colors were unlike anything the track-and-field world had ever seen.

On July 16, 1988, Florence lined up for the qualifying heat of the 100-meter dash. Everyone in the stands was staring at her fluorescent green one-legged suit.

"On your mark, set"—BANG! Florence rocketed out of the blocks and within seconds was ahead of everyone else, her powerful legs propelling her forward. She crossed the finish line in 10.60 seconds, annihilating Evelyn Ashford's world record of 10.76 seconds. No one could believe her time.

Surely the wind must have blown her down the track. Checking the wind gauge, it was confirmed that a 7.15-mile-per-hour wind had been blowing during the race. According to the international rules, world records do not count if there's a wind over 4.47 miles per hour. Florence knew that it wasn't the wind that had made her run so fast. She said, "The 10.60 made me realize I could get into the 10.50s. It made me realize if I kept concentrating, I could go faster."[15]

Two and a half hours later, Florence got ready to race in

the quarterfinals. This time she wore a vibrant plum suit with a turquoise bikini brief. There seemed to be no wind, and she decided that she would show everyone that her first race had not been a fluke. "I had a good start," she said later, "a relaxed middle and kept my knees up at the end. It was more or less a perfect race."[16] Looking up at the clock, she saw the time was an incredible 10.49!

Could it be the wind again? Checking the gauge, the stunned track officials saw it read 0.0! The record stood!

That afternoon Florence went on to easily win the finals of the 100 meters. In the finals of the 200 meters, she came to the starting line in a white lace suit she called an "athletic negligee." At this point, her surprising outfits seemed a fitting complement to her surprising speed. She crossed the finish line in first place with a time of 21.82.

Florence Griffith Joyner was suddenly seen as the United States' best hope for a gold medal in the 100- and 200-meter races. She was invited to be a member of the relay team and this time no one mentioned her long fingernails—the Americans knew they would need her speed! The only thing that dampened her joy at the trials was the fact that Al, competing in the triple jump, failed to make the Olympic team.

After the trials, Florence's success and glamorous style made her an instant superstar. Her picture appeared on the covers of such magazines as *Newsweek* and *Sports Illustrated*. She was inundated by invitations to compete in races all over the world. Also, companies began offering her several hundred-thousand-dollars' worth of endorsements. But Florence and Al turned most of them down.

"Let others chase the fool's gold," Al said. "We'll chase the real gold."[17] To drive home his point, he put the gold medal he had won in the 1984 Olympics around his wife's neck. He said, "When you come back with your three after [the Olympics in] Seoul, you can give me this one back."[18]

By the time she arrived at the airport in Seoul in October

1988, Florence felt confident. But then Al's baggage cart tipped over, landing on her left ankle and injuring her Achilles tendon. Feeling the pain, Florence panicked. Would she be able to race or would all of her hard work be wasted?

While the rest of the athletes spent the final days training on the Seoul track, Florence sat in her hotel room with ice on her leg. By the first day of the track-and-field events, her leg felt strong and she hoped she was ready. When she crouched down at the start of the 100-meter quarterfinals, she was wearing the standard USA track outfit. This time she didn't need any costumes to draw media attention. Everyone was anxious to see how the United States' newest track star would compete against the fastest women in the world.

In the quarterfinals Florence crossed the finish line in first place in a time of 10.62, a new Olympic record. In the semifinals she finished only 0.21 second ahead of the second-place finisher, East German world record holder Heike Dreschler.

In the finals Florence would be running for the gold. This was the moment she had been training for. She would be running against the best sprinters in the world, including Dreschler and Evelyn Ashford. She settled into the starting blocks. Don't tense up, she reminded herself.

When the gun sounded she burst out of the blocks and raced the first 50 meters with her face set in total concentration. But then, as she neared the finish line, a grin of pure joy spread across her face. "I could see that there wasn't anyone at my sides," she said, "so I figured that I was ahead. And it felt so good."[19] Throwing her arms into the air, she leaped across the line to victory. Her time was 10.54 seconds.

Three days later, Florence got ready to run the 200 meters. She was confident of her abilities and hoped to set a new world record. To do so, she would have to beat a time of 21.71 seconds set by Dreschler. In the semifinals she did set a new record of 21.56, but she still had to run the finals. Two hours later she knelt in the starting blocks. *Go hard as I can out of the blocks*, she reminded herself. *Make up the staggers on everybody in the turn. Stay relaxed. Use all I have coming home.*[20]

When the gun went off, she ran fast into the bend of the track. She kept her left shoulder slightly forward to keep from skidding. She was neck and neck with Jamaica's Merlene Ottey, a 1980 and 1984 bronze medalist. Then, as they headed into the straightaway, she pulled away into the lead. When she crossed the finish line, she had broken her own world record with a time of 21.34! Falling to her knees, she kissed the track. When she stood up, she saw Al and cried, "Come here! Come here."[21] Her husband ran over, picked her up and twirled her around and around.

Two days after her victory, the U.S. coaches asked Florence if, in addition to the 400-meter relay, she would run the 1600-meter relay. The coaches hoped her speed would help bring home another Olympic gold. Flattered, Florence agreed.

In the 1600-meter relay, Florence was running the third leg. When her teammate passed her the baton, Florence raced down the track, trying to close a small deficit. As she neared Evelyn Ashford, her team's anchor, Florence nearly ran past her, but managed to hand her the baton just in time. In the last 50 meters Ashford blazed past the competition to victory. For the third time, Florence stood on the champion's podium with a gold medal around her neck. And she still had the 400-meter relay to run! Could she win four gold medals?

Just forty minutes after the first relay, Florence took her place as the anchor runner. Her old rival, Valerie Brisco, would be handing her the baton. When Valerie raced up to her, the United States was only two meters back. Florence fell behind the Soviet runner on the turn, planning to pass her in the straightaway. But when they hit the backstretch, the Soviet runner suddenly blazed ahead. Florence was unable to catch her. To her three golds, Florence added a silver medal.

The next day she said, "Last night I laid out all the medals and I felt that the silver was the special one, because of the team's trust in giving me the chance [to run the 400]. That silver is gold to me."[22]

Her success brought a flurry of awards, including the Sullivan Award, given yearly to the outstanding American amateur athlete. "It's the highest award you can get for your [athletic] accomplishments," Florence said. "It's like the Oscar."[23] She also signed contracts with numerous companies to promote shoes, film, nail products, and toys.

Her success was not completely without a downside, however. For a while Florence was dogged by accusations that she had used performance-enhancing steroids to run so fast. She repeatedly denied the allegations. "I have never used drugs," she said. "I don't believe in drugs, and I'm proud of what I did without drugs."[24] She had never failed a drug test and the claims were never substantiated.

In February 1989, Florence announced her retirement from running. "It's a matter of priorities," she said. "With all I want to do—designing, writing, acting, modeling—I realized there would be no time to train."[25] A few months later, though, Florence admitted, "I miss [running] more than I ever thought I would."[26] She announced a new goal: "I have the dream of running the marathon because I just love running. I'll go out and just run and run and run along the roads. I love the fact of running, and I'm serious about marathons. I hope to run the marathon in the 1996 Olympics."[27]

In her first long-distance race, she ran 5 kilometers in 20 minutes, 30 seconds. Cheering her on as always was husband Al and also her new baby daughter, Mary Ruth.

Although she did not go on to win a spot on the U.S. Olympic marathon team, she said, "I hope people will respect me for trying. As a person and as an athlete."[28]

THREE

JULIE KRONE

The horses burst out of the gates; the crowd jumped to its feet. It was the start of the 1993 Belmont Stakes, one of the biggest events in the world of horse racing. Three quarters of the way through the race, Julie Krone urged her horse, Colonial Affair, forward.

"I threw my reins," she said, "and he sprouted wings. He flew down the stretch, continuing to accelerate as he raced towards the wire."[1]

When she crossed the finish line in first place, Julie Krone became the first woman jockey ever to win the 125-year-old race. Julie looked to the future, vowing, "I don't want to be the best female jockey in the world—I want to be the best jockey."[2]

Born on July 24, 1963, Julie grew up on a farm in Eau Claire, Michigan. She started riding at about the same time she learned to walk. Her mother, an accomplished horsewoman, gave Julie her first pony, Filly. The pony was half Arab, half Shetland, and, Julie joked, "one hundred percent diabolical."[3]

Filly was constantly plotting ways to outwit her young rider. When they went for a walk, Filly would try to buck Julie off or would suddenly sit down on the ground and roll over. Her tricks forced Julie to become a better rider. By the time Julie was five, she was competing successfully in shows.

Julie was not as successful in school as she was in the riding ring. She was a poor speller, and sometimes letters and numbers seemed to jump around on the page when she tried to read them. It wasn't until she was thirty years old that she discovered she had a learning disability called dyslexia.

Ninth grade was especially hard for Julie because her parents were going through an angry divorce. She recalled how "they made a list of all their belongings and divided them in two. . . . They even fought over my bedroom set. . . . What were they planning to do with *me*? Split me in half and each take a portion?"[4] Her father moved out of the house, and Julie's older brother went to live with him. Julie and her mother lived alone on the farm, working with the horses and going to horse shows.

Julie loved to perform tricks on her horse—riding standing up and doing cartwheels over the saddle. She also loved to go fast and would race her horse down the long, empty country roads. When she was thirteen, she watched a jockey win the Belmont Stakes. "I turned to my mom," Julie recalled, "and said, 'I want to be a jockey.'"[5]

At the time, there were few professional women jockeys. The leading woman rider was Patricia Barton. In 1969 she had set a world record by winning 179 races, the most races any female jockey had ever won. "Patti had opened the door [for women jockeys] a crack," Julie said. "Of course, I was determined to bust it off its hinges."[6] One day Julie would do just that—winning more than 3,000 races!

Julie's mother knew it was a long shot but wanted to help

her daughter fulfill her dream. She helped Julie get a summer job working at the Churchill Downs racetrack, home of one of horse racing's biggest events, the Kentucky Derby. There Julie was a "hot-walker," which meant she took care of horses after they had run a race.

Sometimes she was able to convince her boss to let her ride the racehorses on the condition that she would not run them too hard. But as soon as she was out of sight, Julie would hike up the stirrups and urge the powerful horse to go as fast as possible. She would ride hunched over, her hands halfway up the horse's neck, imitating the riding style of the jockeys she watched at the track.

Julie knew that to be a good jockey she would need to be a smart strategist. Watching the races, she noticed how a successful jockey took advantage of a horse's natural strengths and compensated for its weaknesses. The best jockeys would also consider the strengths and weaknesses of the horses they were racing against. For example, if one of the jockeys knew that another horse hated being boxed in, he might try to box that horse in to keep it from running its best.

Julie never worried about getting hurt as a jockey, even though she knew it was a very dangerous sport. Horses can easily bump into each other, or suddenly buck if they become spooked. If one horse trips, it may knock over other horses and riders. When jockeys go down, they are often in danger of being trampled by their own horses or someone else's. Since 1950 at least one hundred jockeys have died from racing injuries and more than fifty jockeys have been paralyzed. [7]

On July 4, 1980, Julie had her first chance to compete in a horse race at a fair. When the starting gates opened, she charged onto the track. She urged her horse forward, saw a break in the pack, broke into that clear space, and crossed the finish line in second place! In another race later that day, she came in first. All summer long Julie raced at the fairgrounds, and every time she rode out onto the track, the stadium announcer would say, "There's Julie Krone, one of the best little jockeys, male or female, we've had at the fair in ages."[8]

When Julie returned for her senior year of high school, she had trouble concentrating in class. All she could think about was the feel of a horse straining forward, the wind in her face as she rounded a turn, the jump of her heart as she galloped toward the finish line. She knew that at her age many jockeys had already started riding professionally. More than anything she wanted to go back onto the track.

In December her mother agreed to let Julie move south to live with her grandparents. There she could work at the Tampa Bay Downs racetrack. Five weeks after she arrived, Julie won her first race. "As we thundered down the stretch I kept thinking, When are all the horses going to pass me? And as I hit the wire, I had to look over my shoulder and double check that I was in front, that no one had slipped by. No one had, and I rode to the winner's circle."[9]

Despite this success, Julie realized that many owners were reluctant to let a girl race their horses. "When I entered the sport," Julie said, "it was almost totally male, and there were definite prejudices among agents, trainers, owners, and jockeys."[10] Many owners and trainers would take one look at little Julie (four-foot-eleven, one hundred pounds) and decide that there was no way she would be strong enough to control their powerful racehorses. In response, Julie developed a bone-crushing handshake.

One trainer later joked, "This cute little girl . . . comes up to me and squeaks, 'Hi! I'm Julie Krone! I'm a jockey!' and takes my hand and *brings me to my knees*. Well, we let her ride, and she rides like a god."[11]

By the end of the season, Julie had raced 48 times, placed first 9 times, second 4 times, and third 10 times. She had also developed a friendship with another woman jockey named Julie Snellings. Snellings no longer rode because she had been paralyzed in a fall, but she gave Julie many valuable riding tips. She also convinced her old agent to let Julie live in his Baltimore house so she could race at the big-league Maryland tracks, including Pimlico. The agent was immediately impressed by Julie's courage and determination. "When she was riding she wasn't reckless," he said. "She was daring. That's the way all the great ones are."[12]

Julie Krone was seventeen years old, living away from home, trying to fight her way to the top in a male-dominated profession. She made some mistakes along the way. During a random drug search of her car in 1980, racetrack officials discovered she had been using marijuana and suspended her from riding for sixty days.

"It was pure torture," Julie said. "I hadn't been off a horse for that long in seventeen years. But I'm glad it happened. It gave me a chance to think about the talent I had been given. I almost threw it away. I was young, but that was no excuse for being stupid."[13]

After the suspension was over, Julie vowed never to use drugs again. Still, her reputation had been damaged and she had even more trouble than before getting mounts.

At a race at Laurel, Maryland, she was thrown from a horse. "I can still remember the feeling of sliding along the dirt, slowing, and then the crushing weight of the horse rolling on top of my body. After that, everything was a blur. I couldn't breathe very well."[14]

Her back was broken. Would she ever be able to ride again? The doctors told her that her only hope was to work hard on her physical therapy exercises. Julie worked so hard that she was back on a horse in an astonishing three months!

After her accident, she failed to win any of her first seventy-nine races. Going into the backstretch of her eightieth race, realizing that she was going to lose again, Julie started screaming, "I quit! I quit! I quit! I can't stand it!"[15] But she did not quit, and won her next race. Her slump was over.

In 1981 she rode more than one hundred winners. In 1982

she moved to the track at Atlantic City, New Jersey. She won more races there than any other jockey, becoming the first woman to win a racing title at a major track. The next year she repeated this feat.

What was it about her that made her so good? In addition to her riding skill and determination, Julie had a special rapport with horses. "Julie truly loves horses," one trainer said. "She talks to them, she sings to them. She moves her little fingers on their necks and they just run like hell for her."[16]

Before a race she would always take the time to get to know her mount, learn what it liked, what made it most comfortable, what made it anxious. "I'll see how he likes to pull," she said. "Does he like to keep pulling or have you let him go? Does he like your hands on or off his neck; which will make him less nervous? And all this you can tell by feel, by what he does with his weight and his head and his mouth."[17]

By 1986 Julie was the number one female rider in the nation, and her horses had won $2.3 million (the jockey receives only 10 percent of the total winnings). Everything seemed to be going her way, until her mother announced that she had cancer. By the time the doctors detected it, the cancer had spread to most of her organs. They gave her a 2 percent chance of surviving. Julie felt frightened, angry, and helpless.

"I would call my Mom and ask if there was anything I could do. She'd always say, 'Yes, win races for me,' in a voice thick with drugs and pain. So I did."[18] Julie mailed her videotapes of her races, and each time she won she'd have a friend call her mother at the hospital to let her know. One time that friend had to call her mother six times as Julie tied the track's record for the most wins in a single day!

When her mother was released from the hospital, Julie bought her a wild stallion to train. She figured that her mother had never given up on any job, so she would have to stay alive to train that horse. She did and eventually was (almost unbelievably) diagnosed as being cancer-free!

Julie, meanwhile, was putting together a string of remarkable accomplishments, including winning back-to-back riding titles at New Jersey's Monmouth Park in 1988 and 1989 and winning the Meadowlands title four years in a row from 1987 to 1990. In 1990 she started racing in New York.

The jockeys in New York were racing for much larger amounts of money, and the competition to get mounts was fierce. Once again Julie found that she had to convince the owners that she was as talented as any male jockey.

"It's a lot tougher as a girl," her agent said, "because if you do something wrong they blow it out of proportion."[19] But Julie was savvy. One expert explained, "She is always [at the track] early, working the horses, and then she'll give the trainers and owners a move-by-move report."[20] She would use her special knack for communicating with the animals to urge them to perform to their peak capacity.

In 1991 all of her hard work paid off when she was asked to ride in the Belmont Stakes. This race, the Kentucky Derby, and the Preakness, constitute the Triple Crown of horse racing. Julie Krone was the first woman to enter the prestigious race. As she said, "To ride onto the track aboard a great horse to the cheers of thousands of fans was overwhelming."[21]

That afternoon Julie finished in ninth place. She vowed to do better in the future. She wasn't satisfied with being the first woman to race in the Belmont Stakes; she wanted to be the first woman to win the Belmont Stakes.

Two years later she felt ready to do just that. Heading for the starting gates, she patted her horse, Colonial Affair, on the neck and whispered, "Let's go and make history, buddy."[22] When the race began, Julie let him drop back a little, then took him wide on the turn. As his hooves thundered over the turf, she kept chanting to herself, "I have a ton of horse, I have a ton of horse."[23] She held him back, waiting for her chance to break free. As they came into the backstretch she kept waiting, and then she saw her opening. She urged the powerful animal forward. He came up alongside the leaders, then broke ahead. That afternoon Julie Krone became the first woman to win the 125-year-old Belmont Stakes and the first woman to win *any* of the Triple Crown races.

By the spring of 1993, she was the first woman to win more than 2,800 races in a career and was one of the top jockeys in the country. Then tragedy struck.

In a race on August 30, 1993, Julie was pulling out of the turn and heading for home when a horse suddenly moved over, blocking her path. Standing up in her stirrups, Julie cried, "No! No!"[24] But her horse was already tripping, sending her flying like a rag doll over its head. "I did a 180," she recalled, "so I was sitting facing the oncoming horses. Pow! I got hit in the heart. My arm was cut so you could see the elbow socket. My ankle hurt so bad I kept thinking, 'Pass out. *Please* pass out!' But I didn't."[25]

Her ankle nearly disintegrated from the impact. She was in excruciating pain and spent three weeks in the hospital. She knew the doctors could not guarantee that her ankle would ever heal completely or that she would be able to race again.

After she left the hospital, she would limp down to the stables in the morning, visit the horses, feed them carrots, breathe in all those familiar smells. In the afternoons she would grit her teeth and undergo painful physical therapy, doing exercises to try to keep her ankle limber. At night she would climb into bed and sob.

By April the doctors announced that she could start riding again. Julie was thrilled, but knew she had a lot of work ahead of her. "I'm going to have to prove myself all over again," she said. "I'm sure there will be people thinking, 'Oh, she's going to be scared now.' With racing, you never rest on your laurels, and there are no counterfeits."[26]

On May 26, 1994, the second day of her comeback, Julie Krone was heading into the homestretch at Belmont Park on her favorite horse, Consider the Lily. They were in second place. Julie held her horse back until she saw the leader sagging; then she let the horse go. Consider the Lily charged into the lead and crossed the line first. In the winner's circle Julie jumped down, pumped her arm into the air, shouting, "Yes! Yes! Yes!"[27] Julie Krone, the champion, was back.

For the next nine months, Julie rode with her customary daring and success. Her horses earned an impressive $3.9 million in winnings. But then, in November 1994, she had to undergo surgery to remove the two metal plates and fourteen screws that had been inserted into her ankle.

While she was recovering, her boyfriend, Matthew Muzikar, a television sports broadcaster, brought her a gift. "I unwrapped this giant box," Julie said, "and there was another little box inside it. Then I unwrapped that and there was another box. . . . It wasn't until I pulled out the last box that a ring popped out."[28]

On January 4, 1995, her ankle had recovered sufficiently for her to start racing at the Gulfstream track in Florida. Within nine days, she was the leading jockey there, winning a total of ten races. But then on Friday, January 13, the horse she was riding snapped its leg and she went flying. Upon landing, she fractured her left hand and wrist. When the doctors told her she would need surgery again, she started crying. "After being back and doing so well and then having it taken away again, it just breaks my heart," Julie said. "I miss the horses already."[29]

In June she returned to racing. She placed second in the 1995 Belmont Stakes. In August she was married, after a full day's racing at the Saratoga track in New York. She continues to be one of the nation's top jockeys. Nothing—not falls, pain, nor fear—keeps Julie from the sport she loves. She has said, "The something inside me that always fought to win, that never gave in to the pain, and that accepted no less than a hundred and ten percent, had never been gone. . . . because that something was simply me."[30]

FOUR

NANCY LOPEZ

Using a swing of tremendous power and accuracy, Mexican American golfer Nancy Lopez became the number one female golfer in the country in her first year as a professional player. She had overcome racial discrimination and financial obstacles to dominate a sport in which most of the previous champions had been privileged white women.

Just about the only person not surprised by Nancy's success was her father. He had taught her to play golf when she was only eight years old and was so confident of her skills that he had built a huge floor-to-ceiling trophy case. "For a while we had to fill in the empty spaces with dishes," Nancy recalled, "but today there's an awful lot of silver in that trophy case!"[1]

Nancy was born in Torrance, California, on January 6, 1957. While Nancy was an infant, her family moved to Roswell, New Mexico, where her father, Domingo, owned and operated an auto-body repair shop. An enthusiastic golfer, he liked to play on the weekends with his wife. Often little Nancy tagged along behind them. When she was eight years old, Domingo handed his daughter a club and told her to hit the ball. "Right away," Nancy recalled, "my ball flew over my parents' heads."[2]

Domingo was thrilled. "I couldn't believe my little daughter could hit the ball so far," he said. "I got excited and told [my wife], 'Maybe Nancy can really play!'"[3] He began coaching his daughter to hit the ball harder and with more accuracy.

In golf, a player starts by hitting the ball as far as possible down the fairway toward the hole. The area around the hole is known as the green. When a player's ball lands on the green, the golfer uses a small, lighter stroke, known as a putt, to get the ball into the hole. The number of strokes an expert golfer is expected to make on each hole is called par. Holes are usually either a par three, four, or five. There are eighteen holes on a standard golf course, and the winner is the person who finishes with the lowest score.

Courses are designed to include tricky holes that test a player's skill. Domingo knew that Nancy would need to learn to make these difficult shots. She would have to learn how to play where the ground sloped, where trees lined the fairways, or where a sand trap or lake bordered the green.

He was confident that if his daughter had time to practice, she might one day be a champion. The only problem was, there was a fee to play on the city course. Domingo did not have enough money to pay for Nancy, his wife, and himself to play. So Nancy's mother made the first of many sacrifices the family would eventually make to further Nancy's career— she quit her beloved game to let her daughter spend more time on the golf course.

As often as possible, Domingo would take Nancy out to practice. By the time she was nine years old, Nancy entered her first Pee Wee golf tournament. She overwhelmed her competition, winning by 110 strokes!

Two years later, she became the youngest player ever to enter the New Mexico Women's Amateur tournament. She lost to the defending champion on the eighteenth hole and finished in second place. Wiping the tears from Nancy's cheeks, Domingo said, "If you want to play good, you have to get beat. That's how you learn."[4] Nancy vowed to get even better and began practicing harder. To pay for her extra hours on the golf course, her father worked overtime and her mother cut corners in the household budget wherever she could.

Nancy tried to make every minute on the golf course count. She said, "You can't just go out and whack balls. Lots of people do that without ever thinking about what they're doing. You have to learn something about yourself and your strokes when you practice, or it's a waste of time. . . . You have to practice your weaknesses."[5]

She concentrated especially on her putting. She had noticed that often the difference between the player who won and those who lost was that the winner consistently sank her putts while the losers occasionally missed. Even after spending hours on the golf course, Nancy would go to the putting green and practice sinking the ball over and over again.

Her hard work paid off. At the age of twelve, she won the New Mexico Women's Amateur Championship, defeating players two and even three times her age! The next year she once again won the tournament.

This sort of success should have automatically given her access to the beautifully manicured and well-designed local country club course. The club had a long-standing policy of allowing talented young players to play without a fee. But because Nancy was Mexican American, the club refused to permit her to play on the course. This discrimination made her more determined than ever to prove she could become a champion.

Later, when Nancy was a national celebrity, she said, "Because I was a Mexican, there were a lot of Anglos in Roswell who weren't ready to accept . . . [me]. Now a lot of them like to say they are my friends. But I don't feel I owe them my friendship because they didn't give me theirs when I was young. My parents gave me all the chances I ever needed."[6]

Nancy also had to battle sexism. At fifteen she was the best young female golfer in the country, having won the United States Golf Association's Girls' Junior Championship. Nevertheless, Goddard High School would not let her play on its golf team because she was a girl! Infuriated, Nancy argued her case before the board of education and forced the school to allow girls to join the team. That year she helped Goddard win the state championship.

Domingo was so proud of his hardworking daughter he bought her a car, a canary yellow sports coupe. When she wasn't practicing golf, Nancy often rode around town in her car, playing the radio and honking the distinctive horn.

The summer after graduating from high school, Nancy played in one of the most prestigious women's golf tournaments in the world, the 1975 United States Open. While the media followed the better-known players, Nancy quietly played a series of very solid rounds and finished in second place.

Fans and journalists crowded around her. Who was this golfing whiz kid? Smiling, Nancy told a throng of journalists, "Right now I just want to enjoy being young, and playing golf as part of my life, but not all of it."[7]

Nancy was looking forward to going to college. She had hoped to go to Arizona State but discovered that although that school gave golf scholarships, it would not give one to a girl. So instead Nancy attended the University of Tulsa, which did offer her a scholarship. Playing on the golf team, traveling to matches, and practicing her swing and putts for hours left her little time to study. After her second year, she made the difficult decision to quit school and become a professional golfer.

In her first three tournaments as a pro, Nancy came in second place each time. Although pleased, she vowed to become number one. Before she could, however, tragedy struck.

Nancy's mother had gone into the hospital for an appendix operation and unexpectedly died. Devastated, Nancy recalled her feelings: "I owed her so much, and I was just on the edge of being able to repay her to some extent for all the years she lavished on me when suddenly she was gone."[8]

Soon after her mother's death, Nancy played in the Bent Tree Classic in Sarasota, Florida. After the first round, she was in third place. After the second round, she was in second place. After the third round, she was tied for first place. In the last round, she pulled into the lead and, weeping most of the way, held onto first place. At the awards ceremony, Nancy dedicated her first professional win to her mother's memory.

That was the beginning of what would turn out to be a red-hot rookie year. By the time Nancy entered the 1978 Ladies Professional Golf Association (LPGA) Championship in Ohio, she had won three tournaments in a row. She was only one win away from tying the record for the most consecutive wins in a season. Suddenly television crews and throngs of fans began following her. Everyone wanted to learn more about the friendly young golfer who had risen to the top of the professional golfing world in her very first season.

The LPGA Championship was one of the most important tournaments. Looking over the course, Nancy was nervous but knew she was hitting the ball well. Also, she had started working with a very good caddie named Roscoe Jones. He did more than just carry her clubs. After Nancy would hit a shot, Roscoe would walk with her to wherever her ball had landed, keeping track of how many steps he had taken. He knew the exact distance he covered with each step and could figure with almost total accuracy how far Nancy had hit the ball.

Nancy and Roscoe then would calculate how many feet she would need to hit the ball again to get it on the green. This helped Nancy determine which club to use. For example, if the ball was 150 feet from the green, Nancy would know to use her seven iron because with that particular club she could usually hit the ball about 150 feet.

At the LPGA Roscoe and Nancy made an amazing team. Over and over again she sent the ball flying perfectly onto the greens. In fact, she was hitting so well that at one point her father shouted from the sidelines, "Nancy, that ball got eyes!"[9] She ended up winning by an astounding six-stroke margin. With her fourth victory in a row, Nancy had tied the record for the most consecutive wins.

The pressure was on—could Nancy break the record? "The other ones I thought, 'If I win, great,'" Nancy recalled. "But the fifth one? I'm very competitive and I wanted to be the only one ever to do it."[10]

On June 11, the day of the tournament, Nancy took deep breaths and tried to remain calm. During the first round she was hitting well, though she knew she could do better. As she neared the end of the course, she hit a long shot that veered off unexpectedly and hit a man on the head! He collapsed, blood dripping down his forehead. Horrified, Nancy rushed over. As she knelt over him, the man smiled weakly and laughed, "At least I'm going to get a chance to meet her!"[11]

Shaken, but relieved that he was not seriously hurt, Nancy went on to play two more good rounds before blasting away her competition in the last round. She had won five consecutive tournaments. The record was hers!

Suddenly Nancy Lopez was a celebrity. Magazines printed articles about her, and everywhere she went people crowded around, asking for her autograph. Companies offered her money to endorse their products, and soon Nancy was doing commercials for orange juice and toothpaste. Despite the public attention, she said, "I'm still a young girl with not too much to be conceited about except that I can hit a golf ball."[12]

A few days before Nancy tried for her sixth straight win, she did an interview with a television sportscaster named Tim Melton. Nancy was struck by his rugged good looks and gentlemanly manner. Although she didn't win the tournament, she did start dating Tim. They were married six months later, on Nancy's twenty-second birthday.

It was a wonderful time in Nancy's life. She finished her rookie year as the number-one female player in the country, winning a total of nine tournaments and a record-setting $189,813 in prize money. She was named the Woman Golfer of the Year, Player of the Year, Rookie of the Year, and was awarded the Vare Trophy, given to the player who turns in the lowest average score for the season.

During the next season Nancy won an impressive eight of the nineteen tournaments she entered. The crowd that followed her along the golf course became known as "Nancy's Navy."

By 1980, however, Nancy and Tim were having difficulties in their marriage. Nancy started having trouble on the golf course as well. The powerful natural golf swing she had used since she was a young girl suddenly became flat and jerky. The ball would shoot off in unexpected directions. "I couldn't hit the ball where I wanted to." Nancy said. "There were times when every day I'd go back to the hotel crying."[13]

In a tournament in Cincinnati, she shot a round that she bitterly described as the worst "since I was a kid. A pudgy, grimy kid."[14] That evening she tearfully called her father and asked him to come out and coach her.

The next day, Domingo stood on the driving range, watching his daughter hit bucket after bucket of balls, giving her a little advice and lots of support. The following day, Nancy's swing was still jerky, but she managed to shoot the second-best round of her career. Afterward, she admitted, "I can't feel excited. . . . There are no guarantees that I'll do it [as well] tomorrow."[15]

She didn't. By the end of the year, Nancy had won only three tournaments. In January, she filed for divorce. "[Tim and I] are just opposites, and I didn't realize it until this past year," she explained. "When I met him I was concerned about finding someone who respected me and wasn't interested in my money. Now I see there are other [important] things in a marriage."[16]

During this difficult time, the person Nancy relied on for support was her friend Ray Knight. Ray was the third baseman for the Houston Astros. Often he and Nancy would chat over cups of cocoa. Nancy said that soon, "we realized that we were alike. He had been devastated [by his own divorce]. So was I. I was playing [golf] poorly, and Ray could relate to that because he went into a hitting slump when he got his divorce."[17]

Ray invited her to spend the winter with him at his parents house in Georgia. Although wary of leaping from one relationship into another, Nancy was falling in love. "I was scared," she said. "But we got along well and we understood each other's feelings about careers."[18] Also, like herself, Ray did not smoke or drink and was deeply religious. Seven months after they started dating, Ray and Nancy were married.

It wasn't long before Nancy was pregnant. On November 7, 1983, she gave birth to their daughter, Ashley. Although she dropped out of the tour early for maternity leave, she was happy again and her golf game had improved.

During the next year, Nancy continued to put aside time for Ashley, playing in only sixteen tournaments, winning two, and finishing seventh on the money list. Even with the help of a nanny, taking care of a baby was hard work. Nancy admitted, "It seemed impossible for me to keep up with the competition. I never thought I would be No. 1 again."[19]

But Ray had different ideas. During the off-season he began pushing his wife to practice more. Often he would go on the golf course and hit balls with her.

"He kept telling me, 'You can be No. 1 if you want to be,'" Nancy said. "The more we played the more he was convinced that I should be No. 1 and that I should rededicate myself."[20]

This is exactly what she did.

In the first three months of 1985, Nancy played well but did not win any tournaments. Then she went on a hot streak, reminiscent of her first two years as a professional. "Maybe I'm playing so well again just because I'm happy," Nancy said.[21] By the end of the season, she had won five tournaments, earned $416,472, and had the lowest scoring average in the history of women's golf. Again she was number one.

She was also pregnant again. In May of 1986 she gave birth to Erin Shea, and by the summer she was playing golf. The next year, Nancy won her thirty-fifth tournament, which qualified her for induction into the LPGA Hall of Fame. This honor has been described as "one of the most difficult attainments in today's world of sports."[22] Only the eleventh woman ever to be so honored, Nancy said, "You think about this day and strive to get to it, but you wonder if it will ever come. This is special."[23]

In 1991 Nancy gave birth to their third daughter, Torri Heather. For a while she considered retiring, but Ray convinced her not to quit playing. "He kicked me out of the house," Nancy laughed. "He told me I still have an outstanding golf game, that I have this talent that I should not squander. So, I got back out and played."[24]

To make sure she had time to spend with her family, she cut back on the number of tournaments she entered and took the children with her whenever possible. Sometimes Ray would come along as well. She admitted, "Now I'm starting to realize [golf] doesn't make me as happy as being with my kids all the time."[25] But Nancy continues to enjoy playing and is still a tough competitor.

The floor-to-ceiling trophy case her father built for her years ago would not be large enough to hold all of the awards she has won over the years. Yet, Nancy says, "I'd love to win a lot more tournaments still. I don't know if I'm going to be capable of winning as many as I'd like because I don't play as much, but I know I can still win. I feel I can."[26]

FIVE

DIANA
NYAD

A world champion marathon swimmer, Diana Nyad swam through shark-infested waters while vomiting and delirious. She endured jellyfish stings, icy water temperatures, and strong, unpredictable ocean currents. In 1979 she set the world record for the longest open-water swim in history for either men or women—eighty-nine miles from Bimini, in the Bahamas, to Jupiter, Florida.

"Marathon swimming is the most difficult physical, intellectual, and emotional battleground I have encountered," Diana said, "and each time I win, each time I touch the other shore, I feel worthy of any other challenge life has to offer."[1]

Born in New York on August 22, 1949, Diana was the oldest of three children. Her parents divorced when she was a toddler, and her mother remarried a Greek land developer whose last name, Nyad, is the water nymph in Greek mythology. Soon after, the family moved to Fort Lauderdale, Florida.

Diana was a particularly energetic and ambitious child. "When I was eight years old," she recalled, "I started getting scared that life was going to be over soon. My only retaliation . . . I felt and still feel, is to be extreme—to do as much as I can and do it as well as possible."[2]

By the time she was ten years old, Diana was becoming a persistent swimmer. Every morning she would wake up at dawn to get ready to swim. As the sky brightened, Diana would be in the pool swimming laps. At lunchtime she would swim sprints. After school she would join the swim team in their two-hour intense workouts. "My mother just thought it was such adolescent eccentric behavior to be crazy about something and to isolate myself," Diana recalled. "I didn't go to birthday parties or movies. I just wanted to swim."[3]

She would swim long after she was exhausted and her teammates had quit for the day. "There is no doubt," she said, "that the overwhelming drive behind my success is that I am absolutely unafraid of pain. I am willing to put myself through anything . . . as long as I can see that the experience will take me to a new level."[4] On her bedroom wall she tacked up a poster that read: There is no gain without pain.

Diana's goal was to swim in the Olympics. By the time she was in the eleventh grade, she had won the backstroke event in six state meets. Then one summer afternoon before her senior year, she suddenly experienced severe chest pains. Her doctor told her that she had contracted a heart virus. After months of bed rest, she realized that the disease had slowed her down. She would never again be a great sprinter. Her dream of competing in the Olympics was dashed.

Frustrated and angry, Diana went off to Emory University in Atlanta, Georgia. Normally a top-notch student, she entered a rebellious phase and was eventually expelled from school after parachuting out of one of the dorm windows.

She spent the following months applying to numerous colleges but was turned down by all of them. Just when she was about to give up hope, she was accepted at Lake Forest College in Illinois. She majored in English and French and earned almost straight A's. While at Lake Forest, the executive director of the International Swimming Hall of Fame, Buck Dawson, urged Diana to try marathon swimming.

There were about seventy men and ten women professional marathon swimmers at that time. For seven months a year they would compete for prize money in long-distance races in places like Egypt, Argentina, and Italy. It was a grueling sport requiring tremendous endurance and physical strength. The athletes would lose, on average, fifteen pounds after a swim. Frequently they would need to be hospitalized because their bodies would go into shock from exhaustion and from spending so much time in freezing waters. The extreme challenge of the sport appealed to Diana.

Her first marathon race was a ten-mile swim across Lake Ontario in 1970. Standing on the shore of the lake, her body covered in grease for warmth, Diana was startled by the size of the swimmers around her. The women's champion was six feet tall and weighed 175 pounds! In contrast, Diana was only five-foot-six and a lean 135 pounds.

When Diana finally reached the opposite shore 4 hours and 23 minutes later, she staggered onto land in tenth place overall and was the first woman out of the water. She had set a new women's world record on her first professional swim!

By 1974 she was the women's world champion and had entered a doctoral program in comparative literature at New York University. She loved marathon competition but felt frustrated by the meager earnings and lack of public recognition. "I once swam a ten-mile race and won $35," she complained.[5]

The final straw came at a race in Buenos Aires, Argentina, in 1975. The winner was guaranteed to receive $3,000. Once the swimmers arrived, however, they discovered that the prize was 3,000 *pesos*—worth about 12¢! "I decided," Diana said, "to take my talent and my experience to some solo swims and to try to make a commercial success of myself."[6] The trick to doing this, she knew, would be to attempt daring swims that would capture media attention. If she could get enough publicity, she could get sponsors and garner high-paying endorsements from companies that wanted her to do commercials for their products.

Diana decided to swim the 26 miles around the island of Manhattan, New York City. She wanted to break the forty-eight-year-old record for the event, held by a man who completed it in 8 hours and 56 minutes. She figured the swim would draw lots of public attention. "The world is four-fifths water," she said, "but the point is to swim where the people are."[7] Manhattan certainly has plenty of people!

The waters, though, were some of the most polluted in the United States. Standing on one of the piers, she could see dead rats and debris floating by in the murky brown water. To protect herself from diseases, Diana had numerous shots. Still, her doctor warned her that there was no guarantee she wouldn't contract some other virus.

She began putting in long hours at the pool, going for twelve-mile jogs, and playing squash. She found it difficult to keep her weight up and would eat 12,000 calories a day—about 10,000 more than the average woman! All day long she gulped down raw eggs, raw steaks, and raw vegetables because, she said, "its easier than cooking."[8]

Eight days before her race around Manhattan she began an intense study of the currents. She knew she would have to navigate through the whirlpools known as Hell Gate, which had sucked boats under water and then spit them back up hundreds of feet away. She decided she would attack these first, when she was at her strongest. A support team would follow her in a boat to give her high-energy feedings every hour.

On September 24, 1975, Diana dove into the muck and headed toward Hell Gate. Only a few reporters were there. Maybe, Diana hoped, there would be more media attention when the swim was over. She made it easily through Hell Gate and reached the tip of Manhattan at dusk, right on schedule. New Yorkers gathered along the shore to watch her swim past and cheer encouragement.

The water was getting choppier due to a hurricane that had swept the Northeast, and as the sky darkened, the waves began hitting Diana hard in the face. Rain came slashing down. The current was too strong to swim against and the water was getting colder and colder.

Diana began dog-paddling, desperately hoping the current would shift. Boats chugged toward her, unable to see her in the dark. The support boat flashed its spotlights, trying to keep them away. Still the current wouldn't change. Diana hung on for another hour, but it was hopeless. When she was finally pulled from the water, she was deathly pale. "So cold, so cold . . ." she mumbled, her body shivering uncontrollably.[9]

The news media converged on her at the hospital. Television cameras focused on the twenty-five-year-old swimmer shivering in the hospital bed, fighting her way back. An hour later Diana was sitting up, vowing to try again.

She did. For her second attempt on October 6, the media were there in full force—television crews lining the seawall. This time, all of New York City seemed to be rooting for Diana Nyad. When she finally emerged from the water at the end of the 26 miles, she had a new record—7 hours and 57 minutes.

She was interviewed by all three major television networks and numerous magazines. Her photo was on the front page of the *New York Times*. She was offered a job as a sports announcer, promised $75,000 in endorsements, and given a contract to write a book about her experiences. She was finally reaping considerable financial rewards from her swimming.

Diana decided her next big challenge would be to cross the English Channel. It was said to be the toughest long-distance swim because not only were the channel's currents unpredictable but also the water was extremely cold, its temperature averaging at 58°F. Only 20 percent of the 1,100 people who had attempted the crossing had succeeded.

With her typical zeal, Diana decided that she would not only swim across the channel, but she would then return. If she succeeded, she would be the first woman ever to complete a double crossing. "I am simply not given to understatement," she admitted. "My world view is dramatic."[10]

Diana made three valiant attempts at this swim. The first time she had to quit after becoming seasick and vomiting up her feedings. The second time the waves were too high and the swells made swimming impossible. The third time the water was too cold, and Diana had to be pulled out when her body temperature dropped so low she began turning blue.

Returning to America, she realized, "It is . . . so easy to walk away from victory swelling with pride and optimism, believing unswervingly in yourself. Walking away from defeat the same way is a true challenge."[11]

Undeterred, she began planning a new swim. "I want to do something unprecedented in the world of sports," she said. "Something so outrageously difficult it would go unmatched for many, many years to come."[12] She decided to make the longest open-water swim ever—130 miles, demanding about sixty hours of continuous swimming, from Cuba to Florida. It would require astounding physical and mental strength.

In her book *Other Shores*, Diana described the surprising mental impact of solo marathon swimming. For mile after mile, hour after hour, she performed the same movements over and over—stroking, kicking, breathing. It was unbelievably boring. To keep occupied, she used to count her strokes—six hundred strokes equaled a mile. Sometimes she would count to "Row, Row, Row Your Boat" and other songs.

After swimming a long time, she said she would lose her grip on reality and no longer be able to count her strokes. Then her body would move on autopilot while her mind would drift and she would have strange visions.

"I [would] feel exactly as though I am in the middle of a night dream," she said, "in a hallucination beyond my control."[13] Once she imagined that there were seagulls attacking her. Another time she relived childhood memories. These fantasies would feel incredibly real to her. She would flail around in the water, attacking imaginary birds or talking to invisible people. She felt these hallucinations helped her know herself better. They let her tap into her subconscious mind.

She believed the hallucinations resulted not only from extreme physical exhaustion but also from the lack of normal sensory input she would experience on long swims. She could not see because her goggles would fog up; she could not hear because her swimming cap covered her ears. Her senses of touch, taste, and smell would be distorted by the water. The strongest stimulation she experienced were her thoughts. Under such conditions her mind would wander out of her conscious control.

Diana knew that on her swim to Florida she would probably become delirious. She said, "I imagine myself in the fifty-ninth hour. . . . I'll be delirious . . . thinking I can't make it. Crying and throwing off my goggles, and having tantrums . . . realizing I don't want to do this. . . . It's too hard. . . . And then in the middle of that tantrum, I see the Florida coast. . . . It seems as though it will take me another sixty hours, but it doesn't matter. . . . As long as you can see the end, you know you're going to get there. No matter how slowly you go."[14]

She began training for the swim a year in advance. For the first six months she worked out on land—running, playing squash, and lifting weights. The last six months she swam for up to twelve hours a day. When she wasn't working out, she was gathering publicity, putting together a support team, and rounding up $150,000 in cash for her endeavor. With $65,000 of that money, she commissioned a gas-powered 20-by-40-foot shark cage in which to swim.

She originally hoped to swim during the gentle month of

July, but problems with the Cuban government delayed the swim until August 13, 1978. At two o'clock in the afternoon she waded into the waters off Ortegosa Beach, Cuba, and waved good-bye to her friends and the large crew of journalists covering the event. "I guess I'll see you all in about two and a half days," she shouted before diving in.[15]

Soon it became clear that her expensive shark cage was making swimming difficult. It trapped the swells, sending the waves crashing mercilessly into her, then bouncing backward, creating a double-wave effect. As the size of the waves increased toward evening, Diana became seasick and began vomiting her high-protein feedings.

Her navigators steered her farther west to allow her to swim more parallel to the waves. This was a fateful decision, putting her far off course. In the night Diana swam into a school of jellyfish, screaming as they stung her.

"My God," she cried. "This is the worst night of my life."[16]

As dawn broke she began to hallucinate that there were barracudas at the bottom of the cage. She was off course, miles from land, a lone swimmer in vast open sea. By nightfall the swells were up to seven feet. Exhausted, her lips swollen from the seawater, Diana thought her cage was a cave. By the next morning her team had to admit the swim was hopeless.

She was 70 miles from Cuba's coast when her trainer leaned overboard and said, "Diana, we are off course."

"You mean I have to swim another twenty hours to reach Florida?" Diana asked. "I can do it."

"No, Diana, you couldn't reach Florida if you swam fifty more hours."[17]

They pulled Diana onto the boat, her skin pale, her eyes glassy. "I never did anything so hard in my life," she whispered. "No swimmer in the world could have done what I did."[18]

Disappointed but not defeated, Diana decided to swim from the Bahama Islands to Florida. Another swimmer, Stella Taylor, had unsuccessfully attempted this feat four times.

Though not as long as the Cuba-Florida swim, it would still be the longest open-water swim ever. This time Diana would have the proper navigational equipment to keep her on course.

On her first attempt she was stung and paralyzed by a Portuguese man-of-war. After a two-week recovery, she was ready to try again. On August 19, 1979, she waded into the warm, green water of the Bahamas. Scuba divers rode on the support boat and regularly dove into the water to check for sharks, jellyfish, and the dreaded man-of-war. Once they spotted a mako shark, and the support boat set off the electronic shark shield. It sent out a wave of electricity that irritated the shark but didn't affect Diana. The mako disappeared.

"We would look back at Diana, plugging along at her incessant 54-40-55 strokes a minute," one observer on the boat said,"and realize how frail and exposed she actually was."[19]

As dawn began to break, she could see the shore. News helicopters were thundering overhead. Diana kept swimming at the same pace she'd kept up for almost twenty-eight hours. As she staggered up on the Florida beach, her eyes and lips were swollen grotesquely, but she grinned for the cameras. She knew she had made history.

After that she retired from marathon swimming and became a sports announcer for ABC. She said, "I think that early on ABC appreciated the fact that I can formulate thoughts quickly and ad lib if necessary."[20] She has covered events for *Wide World of Sports* and other specials such as the Ironman Triathlon competition. She has also written two books, *Other Shores* and *Diana Nyad's Basic Training for Women*. She continues to give motivational speeches to college students and corporations.

"My life has never been better," Diana has said. "All the vitality I put into and got out of swimming can go into everything else."[21]

SIX

JOAN
BENOIT SAMUELSON

In 490 B.C. a long-distance runner left the site of a great battle in Marathon, Greece, for the capital, Athens. Scrambling over the rocky land, he raced 26 miles, 365 yards, to bring the glorious news to his country's leaders that the Greek armies had vanquished the Persians. Most modern-day marathons cover this same distance. They are one of the most strenuous events in contemporary sports, testing an athlete's endurance and courage. One of the greatest women marathoners of recent times is Joan Benoit Samuelson. She has said, "The sport has been good to me, especially in that it has given me the chance to test the limits of my ability and find the strength of my heart."[1]

Joan Benoit was born on May 16, 1957. She grew up in Cape Elizabeth, Maine, with two older brothers and one younger brother. She always wanted to prove that she was their equal in every way, including in sports. One of her family's favorite sports was skiing. Joan loved the exhilaration of racing down a mountain and the feel of the wind in her face. She dreamed of being good enough to ski in the Olympics. To do so she knew she would have to train hard and often force herself to go on another run even after she was completely exhausted.

Her parents didn't want Joan to focus exclusively on athletics and taught her that there were many other important things in life, including schoolwork and church. Still, all winter long, they allowed Joan and her brothers to go to mass bundled up in ski clothes so that afterward they could immediately head to the slopes.

Sometimes Joan competed in ski races. Her father recalled, "Her first race was a little thing, only halfway down the bunny slope. Joanie won. She was only in the third grade, but you could see the exhilaration in her face."[2]

Joan brought this desire to excel to the other sports she enjoyed—tennis, field hockey, basketball, and, of course, running. During her freshman year of high school, she had already started running eight or nine miles on the weekends. During the field hockey season, while her teammates limped off the field after practice, she would sprint around the track for a few more miles, forcing her body to the limits of endurance. "I liked pushing myself to keep going after exhaustion set in," she said. "It was a game I played [with myself]."[3]

Still, her first love was skiing and might have remained so if she hadn't suffered a serious fall during her sophomore year. Joan had been practicing all day on a slalom course and, although she was tired, she wanted to try once more to ski it perfectly. As she zigzagged between the flags, she suddenly lost her concentration and slammed into one of them. She heard her leg pop and knew she was badly injured. At the hospital, the doctor confirmed that it was broken.

It wasn't until the next winter, when she stood at the top of a mountain looking down, that she realized she would never again be able to attack a course with complete assurance. Never again would she be so aggressive on the slopes. "The leg would mend," Joan said, "but the part of me that didn't hold anything back when I was on the slopes was permanently damaged. I had lost my nerve. Without it, I'd never be a great skier."[4] After that, she began concentrating on field hockey and running.

At the time, she never considered becoming a professional athlete. "It was difficult to imagine a career in athletics when there wasn't so much as an organized team for girls below high school age in my hometown," Joan said. "And, yes, even as I got older, I had to operate more on faith than on any evidence that things were going to change for women athletes. Where boys my age could realistically aspire to professional careers in any number of sports, my role models [as a girl] were few, and my opportunities were severely limited."[5]

After graduating from high school in 1975, Joan attended Bowdoin College in Brunswick, Maine. Since Bowdoin didn't have a women's track team, she made field hockey her college sport, though she did continue to run extra miles after practice. On the weekends she entered as many races as possible.

During her sophomore year, she angered her field hockey coach by running in a half-marathon on Sunday, placing second, and then being too tired to play in their field hockey game on Monday. At the end of the season she decided it was time to admit to herself that she loved running more than field hockey. After that, she dedicated herself to becoming the best runner she possibly could.

She would join the men's cross-country team on their ten-mile loops, logging up to fifty miles a week. "When I think back," Joan said, "I see myself studying or running all the time. I don't remember goofing off with my friends very much, which is something I regret."[6] This dedication earned her high grades and top finishes in numerous road races that drew the attention of track coaches from around the country. North Carolina State University offered her a full-year's scholarship if she would agree to run for their team. The offer was tempting. Bowdoin was an expensive school, there was no women's track team, and Joan longed to train with an experienced coach. She decided to spend her junior year in the South at North Carolina State University.

It would prove to be a difficult time. "I'm a Yankee," she said. "I missed Maine. I missed the ocean."[7] In the middle of the track season, Joan contracted mononucleosis, a disease that causes extreme exhaustion. She was too sick to run for North Carolina State, which made her feel guilty about taking its scholarship money. But, after returning to Maine for the summer, she decided to go to the South for one more semester. She helped the team come in second place in the national track meet, and Joan was awarded All-American honors. That fall she set a record in a 10K (10-kilometer) race, and the Nike Corporation started sponsoring her.

She entered her first full-length marathon soon after. She had flown to Bermuda to race in a 10K, which she won, and stayed to watch the marathon. A friend suddenly turned to her and said, "Hey, why don't we enter the marathon?"

Joan laughed. She had never run twenty-six miles before. But then she thought, why not? What did she have to lose? She would run as far as she could and drop out when she had to.

Minutes before the race began, Joan rushed up to the registration desk, grabbed a number, and went to the starting line. Racing in the light rain, Joan kept passing the other runners. Although she felt tired, she kept pushing ahead. "Before I knew it I had overtaken all but one of the women," she said.[8] She finished her first marathon in 2:50:54 (2 hours, 50 minutes, 54 seconds), a time good enough to qualify her for the prestigious 1979 Boston Marathon!

Back at Bowdoin, Joan was not only becoming more serious about her running, she was also becoming serious about her boyfriend, Scott Samuelson, a lanky psychobiology major and pole-vaulter on the track team. "We started to call each other M.D., for Major Distraction," Joan remembered.[9] Nevertheless, she managed to concentrate on her training for the Boston Marathon and, on the day of the race, felt like she was fully prepared and anxious to begin.

Then, on her way to the marathon, Joan was stuck in a traffic jam. "I just got out of the car and ran through the woods," she recalled. "I must have bushwhacked two miles to the start."[10] Wearing a Bowdoin jersey, she focused on hitting her stride right from the beginning. It wasn't until the last third of the race that she took the lead. "I knew the TV cameras were trained on me from about mile eighteen on and I realized something special was happening."[11]

When she crossed the finish line in 2:35:15 no one could believe it. A little-known college student had won the Boston Marathon and set a new American and course record for women! Joan was instantly swamped by the media and fans. Charities began asking her to attend their fund-raisers and the phone always seemed to be ringing. Even President Jimmy Carter invited her to the White House for dinner. The attention was overwhelming.

After the Boston Marathon, Joan Benoit raced in many places, including New Zealand, France, and Italy. She didn't always feel in peak condition, however. After a race in Florida she felt so sick that she was admitted to the hospital and diagnosed as having appendicitis that required surgery. Soon after, she had a small noncancerous cyst (lump) removed from under her arm. These surgeries kept her from being able to defend her title in the Boston Marathon in 1980, and in 1981 she placed a disappointing third.

During this time her heels also were often sore, sometimes becoming so inflamed she couldn't walk. Finally she decided to undergo a somewhat risky surgery to correct the problem. She said she knew that "either my feet wouldn't heal properly and I'd have to stop running or they would be fine and I could do what I liked."[12]

Luckily her feet healed quickly. In the first marathon she entered after surgery, she set a new American record, finishing the course for the first time in less than 2 hours, 30 minutes!

Joan was back in tip-top form and vowed that she would win the 1982 Boston Marathon. At the starter's gun, she zoomed out at a sprint, feeling strong, and took the lead. Her stride was short but fast and very fluid. No one could catch her. The television announcers wondered if she would be able keep up this pace, or if she might burn out toward the end.

She recalled that as she neared the finish, "My legs wobbled alarmingly on one downhill stretch and I thought maybe that was the end, but the finish line was close, now, and I couldn't give up. I recovered my composure."[13] She staggered across in 2:22:43, setting a new world record.

Instead of taking a break and resting on her laurels, Joan headed back to Maine to start training for the Olympic trials. The International Olympic Committee had announced that for the first time ever there would be a women's marathon included in the Olympic Games. Remembering her childhood dream of participating in the Olympics, Joan wanted to run in that race. To make the American team, she would have to place in the top three at the trials, which were scheduled to be held in Olympia, Washington, on May 12, 1984.

Joan felt confident she would make the team. Her training was going well and she felt stronger than ever. Also, she had bought a beautiful old house on the Maine coast that she enjoyed remodeling. In the afternoons, Joan would pick berries to make into jelly. She felt contented and at peace.

But then, on a routine jog through the beautiful countryside, she felt something in her knee clench and stiffen. Panic gripped her. What was wrong? Seventeen days before the Olympic trials, Joan discovered that she would have to undergo knee surgery. She knew the chances of her competing in the trials were slim, but forced herself not to lose hope. It was hard. She said, "A week before the marathon, I couldn't even climb into the stands to watch a track meet. I could not run a step. I couldn't do anything."[14]

Then the knee began to heal and she started to run again. Favoring that leg, she pulled a hamstring in the other leg. Now, she thought, fighting back tears, it wasn't her knee that was going to keep her from competing, but her pulled muscle.

Still, she refused to give up. Three days before the trials, she gritted her teeth and told herself, "This is it. You have to go out and run at least 15 miles. If you can't, there's no way you're going to run in the trials."[15] That afternoon, ignoring the pain of her hamstring, she ran sixteen miles.

On the day of the trials, her boyfriend from Bowdoin, Scott Samuelson, showed up in Washington to cheer her on. Joan vowed to finish the race. "I just wanted to be able to cover the distance," she said. "I didn't care how fast I ran."[16]

On May 12, 1984, Americans witnessed the profound courage and tremendous inner strength of Joan Benoit. Not only did she complete the marathon trial, she won it. Crossing the finish line, she broke into sobs.

By the time of the Olympic Games, her knee and hamstring had healed and she felt in good shape. That year the games were being held in Los Angeles, California. During opening ceremonies, standing with all the other athletes in the coliseum stadium, watching the Olympic torch being lit, Joan said, "I had the shakes as I realized where I was. . . . To call these minutes electric would be to understate the case; my whole body was tingling with awe and pride."[17] She had overcome so much to arrive at this moment and yet knew her greatest challenge still lay ahead. She would be competing against the best marathon runners in the world.

Sunday, August 5, 1984, Joan joined the rest of the marathoners at the start of the race. Her heart was pumping hard. When the starter's gun went off, she jumped into the lead. "I couldn't believe the other runners weren't coming after me," she said. "I glanced over my shoulder a few times . . . but no one appeared."[18] All of her training was paying off. She listened to her feet hitting the pavement, concentrated on keeping her strides even. The television truck rumbled along in front of her, the cameras focused on her face. Every few miles she'd glance back and every time she'd see that no one was near.

As she left the final street and approached the coliseum stadium with its finish line, she passed a mural that had been painted on the side of a building. It showed her breaking the tape at the Boston Marathon. She grinned and ran past it.

Running into the tunnel leading into the Coliseum, she could hear the thundering applause of the crowd. Her dream had come true! Joan Benoit had won the Olympic gold medal. An American flag was shoved into her hands, and she ran once more around the track, letting it unfurl.

Suddenly Joan Benoit was a media celebrity. She appeared on television shows and at charity functions. She said, "My life had been active before, but never to this extent."[19] Traveling all over the country to accept awards and make appearances, her training was inconsistent and 1985 was a difficult year. She placed a discouraging eleventh in a minimarathon, but then won the important Chicago Marathon.

Joan married Scott Samuelson and gave birth to two children, Abigail and Anders. "Running used to be my life focus," she said. "But with motherhood came duties that affected my desire to put a lot of time into training."[20] If she thought running a marathon was tough, she discovered that raising two children was even tougher. "[Motherhood] never stops," she said, "whereas 26 miles has a beginning and an ending."[21]

Although she would have liked to compete in the 1988 Olympics, she could not because she was having trouble with her Achilles tendon. In the 1989 Boston Marathon she finished a frustrating ninth. Soon after, she was diagnosed with chronic asthma, which made it hard for her to breathe. In 1992 she again decided that she wasn't ready to run in the Olympics.

At the 1993 Boston Marathon she said, "I lost the race at 9:00 A.M. I was dizzy the day before in the humidity. I thought, 'You're the mother of two. Do you want to put your life in jeopardy?'"[22] She kept herself from pushing too hard and finished in sixth place.

Despite these disappointing finishes, Joan still felt she could run a marathon in less than 2 hours and 20 minutes, and she set her sights on competing in the 1996 Olympic Games which were being held in Atlanta, Georgia. She said the first step would be to run the 1994 Chicago Marathon in under 2 hours and 42 minutes, the time required for a berth in the Olympic trials.

The morning of the race she said, "I hugged my kids before I went out the door. It was like going to war. I didn't know if I was going to make it."[23] That afternoon, at the age of thirty-seven, this mother of two finished the race in 2:37:09, placing sixth and earning a spot at the trials. To actually make the Olympic team, she would have to place in the top three at the trials in Columbia, South Carolina..

On February 10, 1996, she joined 187 other runners at the start of the hilly course. She said, "It would mean a lot to me to make a U.S. Olympic team and compete here in the States 12 years after my first."[24] But when she crossed the finish line, she was in thirteenth place with a time of 2:36:54.

Although she did not make the 1996 Olympic team Joan Benoit Samuelson has left her mark on long-distance running. As she has pointed out, it wasn't so long ago that "conventional wisdom held that women were too frail and delicate to run more than a few thousand meters. . . . The underlying message, of course, was that running, and athletics in general, were unfeminine. I heard that loud and clear as a teenager."[25] With grace and dignity, Joan Benoit has helped to end that myth, proving just how far and how hard a woman can run.

SEVEN

Monica Seles

On April 30, 1993, tennis star Monica Seles was brutally stabbed during a match in Hamburg, Germany. At the time, the nineteen-year-old was the number-one ranked female player in the world. Her physical injuries healed quickly, but the emotional scars remained. Some wondered if she would ever return to the sport.

But two years after the attack, Monica walked back into the spotlight to a standing ovation. Since then, her courageous comeback and return to her sport have won the hearts and respect of tennis fans all over the world.

She has said, "I don't just want to be the one who got stabbed. I want to be remembered for my game, and I want to give something back to the game. . . . There's still a lot I want to accomplish."[1]

Monica Seles did not become an American citizen until 1994, though she has spent most of her tennis career living in the

United States. She was born on December 2, 1973, in Novi Sad, the Hungarian section of Yugoslavia. Her mother, Esther, was a computer programmer and her father, Karolj, a documentary filmmaker and renowned cartoonist. Karolj had a bachelor's degree in physical education.

Karolj began teaching Monica to play tennis when she was six years old. He encouraged his small, left-handed daughter to use an unorthodox double-handed forehand as well as a double-handed backhand. This allowed her to hit the ball very hard from either side. To make practicing more fun, he would sometimes draw Tom and Jerry cartoons on the balls. Other times he'd give her rewards. "If I hit five balls into a box," Monica remembered, "I got a Barbie."[2]

It wasn't long before Monica loved the game so much she did not need any incentives to practice. Day after day she would go out on the courts and hit backhands, forehands, volleys, lobs. She developed tremendous control for such a young player and could make the ball spin, drop short, or land in a corner. She liked to stay near the back of the court and make her opponent run to return her varied shots.

At eight, Monica was so good she won her country's competition for youngsters twelve and under. "She didn't know the rules," her older brother, Zoltan, said. "She was playing the points and not counting. She was always asking me whether she was winning or losing."[3]

Tennis is scored on three levels: points, games, sets. When a player wins enough points, she wins a game. When she wins six games by a margin of two, she wins a set. To win a tournament, she usually must win two out of three sets in the final match. To get to the finals, she usually must defeat players in at least two previous matches.

When Monica was ten, she won the European junior championships and in 1985 became the youngest person ever to win the Sportswoman of the Year Award in Yugoslavia.

Soon after she caught the eye of a tennis coach named Nick Bollettieri. He ran a prestigious tennis academy in Bradenton, Florida. Bollettieri recalled, "I was so impressed that I offered Monica a full scholarship and invited the entire family to come and live at the academy."[4]

Monica spent the next two years practicing tennis for five to eight hours a day. Sometimes she hit the ball so hard her racket would break. Often Bollettieri had to restring four rackets a week for her!

There were no girls at the academy who could hold their own against Monica, so she would play with her brother, Zoltan, (also a Yugoslavian junior champion) or other boys at the academy.

Sometimes Bollettieri would encourage Monica to take a day off, but she always refused. "I just love to play and practice," she said. "I love to learn new things. I get excited about getting better and making changes in my game."[5]

In 1987 Monica made her professional debut at the Virginia Slims Tournament in Florida, where she lost in the second round. Two years later she competed against the number-one-ranked (or "seeded") player, Chris Evert, at the Virginia Slims tournament in Houston. A virtually unknown underdog, Monica fell behind Chris and then rallied. She slammed her two-handed shots past her veteran opponent to win her first professional championship.

During 1989 she competed in some of the biggest tennis tournaments in the world, including the so-called Grand Slam which consisted of tournaments known as the French Open, Australian Open, U.S. Open, and Wimbledon. Although she did not win any of these big events, she reached the quarterfinals in eight out of the ten tournaments she entered and rose from being ranked eighty-sixth in the world to sixth. One expert said, "Pound for pound, she hits the ball harder than anyone I've ever seen. . . . She's a commando on a search-and-destroy mission."[6] Monica Seles appeared to be on the verge of becoming one of the top three women players in the world.

At the beginning of 1990, however, Monica entered a slump. She seemed awkward on the court and her swing was less fluid. She had suffered a minor injury to her shoulder, but the real problem seemed to be coming from a growth spurt. She had grown six inches in one year (from five-foot-three to five-foot-nine)! "When I looked at the court the angles were all so different," she explained.[7] With her new height came new strength. "The racket seemed lighter," she said, "like I was playing Ping-Pong."[8]

During this difficult period, Monica's parents felt that Bollettieri should spend more time working with their daughter, but he had obligations to other players as well, including future superstar Andre Agassi.

By March Monica had regained control of her game and was hitting harder than ever. Her serve was clocked at a devastating 103 miles per hour!

After winning the Lipton International Players Championship, she felt it was time to leave Bollettieri's tennis academy. Her father became her sole coach.

In 1990 Monica began an astounding ascent to the top of the professional tennis world. She began by beating number-two-ranked Martina Navratilova at the Italian Open. It was an experience that Navratilova compared to being run over by a truck. [9] A few days later, at the German Open, Monica stunned fans by beating the number-one-ranked player in the world, Steffi Graf. Until then, Graf had won sixty-six matches in a row.

Fans were thrilled when Monica and Steffi met again in the finals of the prestigious French Open. Would Steffi be able to put the young upstart with the double-fisted hits and Woody Woodpecker laugh back in her place?

When the coin was tossed at the start of the 1990 French

Open, Monica won and made the decision to let Steffi serve first. Most top-level players tend to win their serves, but Monica wanted to show Steffi just how confident she was.

When Steffi's serve whizzed across the net, Monica was ready. She sent it blistering back into Graf's court. After a hard-fought first game, Monica was on top, the crowd thundering its approval. This was tennis at its best. Two tremendous competitors, giving it their all.

By the time Monica was ahead three games to one, it was raining and the officials called time-out for almost an hour. After the break, Graf fought back strongly, but Monica did not give up. She won the set, the match, the tournament. She became the youngest woman to win a Grand Slam event in 103 years and proved that her previous victory over Steffi was no fluke.

It was clear that a new rivalry was forming between Graf and Seles. Before Monica burst onto the scene, Steffi Graf was regularly out-playing all of her other competitors (including Navratilova, who was nearing her midthirties and preparing to retire). But now it was clear that Monica was going to challenge Steffi for every win.

Going into the U.S. Open, Monica had taken over the number two ranking from Navratilova, and if she could beat Steffi again, she would have a chance to unseat her as number one. But Monica disappointed fans by losing in the third round of the U.S. Open to a player ranked eighty-second in the world.

Still, by the end of 1990, Monica had won 54 out of the 60 matches she played, including 9 tournaments. She had earned $1.63 million in prize money and $6 million in endorsement contracts.

Monica began 1991 by winning both the Australian and French Opens. She boosted Steffi out of first place after 186 weeks of being number one. At seventeen, Monica became the youngest player ever to earn this ranking. "Sometimes I wish I could have waited three of four years to become No. 1," she later admitted. "I would have had a little more time to . . . prepare for how to handle myself."[10]

One of the things she would later wish she could have handled better was her decision to pull out of Wimbledon. Fans had been eagerly anticipating the tournament because Monica would be competing for her third straight Grand Slam of the year. But three days before the start of the tournament, she mysteriously withdrew and disappeared from public view without a clear explanation. Rumors abounded.

Twenty-seven days later, Monica held a massive press event. She climbed out of a white limo (imitating her idol, Madonna,) wearing a wig and carrying her little dog. She told the throng of journalists that she'd had shinsplints and a stress fracture in her left leg. Although her reason for dropping out of the tournament was valid, the publicity stunt was seen by some as a tasteless example of how fame had gone to her head.

One reporter said, "Seles . . . was really too much, batting her eyes . . . and affecting a breathy voice—you expected her to call you 'dahling' at any moment."[11] Monica later said, "I wish people would forget about it. It wasn't the best experience."[12] Nevertheless, by the end of the year, no one could dispute Monica's talent. She had won every Grand Slam she entered and earned $2.4 million.

In 1992 she reclaimed her Australian Open title and was the favorite going into the French Open. There, she met Steffi Graf in the final. Monica played aggressively from the baseline. She won the first set, but Steffi fought back and captured the second set. In the final, Monica came from behind to win. Seles and Graf had played all-out for 2 hours and 43 minutes. Both women were so exhausted they could barely stay on their feet long enough to shake hands. Monica would go on to win every other 1992 Grand Slam except for Wimbledon, insuring her right to remain number one.

She began the 1993 season where she had left off the year before, winning the Australian Open. But then Monica caught a bad viral infection and had to miss all the tournaments from late February until April.

When she was finally feeling better, she flew to a tournament in Hamburg, Germany. On April 30, 1993, she was ahead of Bulgarian player Magdalena Maleeva, 6-4, 4-3. Sitting down on the bench during a break, she leaned forward, wiped her face, told herself to keep concentrating.

Suddenly she felt a sharp pain in her upper back. Turning around, she saw a man gripping a knife. Screaming, Monica stumbled forward toward the net. Security guards grabbed her attacker as she collapsed on the court. Horrified fans watched as blood seeped through her white tennis shirt. The blade had narrowly missed hitting her spinal cord, which could have paralyzed her.

The attacker was a thirty-eight-year-old unemployed East German named Gunther Parche. He was obsessed with Steffi Graf and, as a police spokeswoman explained, "[He] said quite clearly that he did not want to kill Monica Seles. He only wanted to injure her and make her unable to play so that Steffi Graf could become number one again."[13]

The next morning Steffi Graf rushed to the hospital to visit Monica. "I told her I am very sorry," Graf said, her eyes filling with tears. "I felt incredibly bad. We could hardly speak."[14]

When Monica was released from the German hospital, she went to a sports medical facility in Vail, Colorado. There she discovered that the pain of the stabbing was not only physical but also emotional. She often had nightmares, reliving the attack. She would hear herself screaming. "My scream is what stayed with me a long time," she said. "It was eating me alive. . . . I pretty much moved to daylight sleeping times. I couldn't sleep at night. I saw shadows in every corner."[15]

From May to September she stayed in seclusion in Vail,

working on her physical therapy exercises to try to limber up the damaged back muscles.

In the fall she returned to her house in Sarasota, Florida. "I began hitting balls," she said. "My dad threw them at me at first, and I got mad because that seemed like an insult. He was very patient and I wasn't."[16] During this time she couldn't bear to watch any televised tennis matches because all she could think about was how she should be there.

One of the things that helped her work through the emotional trauma of the knifing was being able to talk to other victims of violent crimes via a Florida-based telephone support network. "They aren't celebrities, or anything like that," Monica said, "just people who share one thing—having been stabbed."[17] It helped her to be able to call these people at any time during the day or night and discuss her feelings.

She also started working out with Olympic track star Jackie Joyner-Kersee. "Being anywhere near her is inspiring," Monica said. "I mean I'd glance at her and think, Well, if *she* can force herself to do another sit-up, I can, too."[18]

While Monica was recovering in Florida, her assailant was being put on trial in Germany. Monica decided not to attend the proceedings after she discovered that the layout of the court meant that she would have to sit with her back to her attacker. The judge decided on October 14, 1993, that her attacker should be given a two-year suspended sentence and released on parole. The judge said that she found his promise not to hurt anyone again "absolutely believable."[19]

Hearing the verdict, Monica was shocked and horrified. "They say he doesn't have to go to jail at all? I don't understand," she sobbed. "I'm . . . just . . . so . . . confused."[20] Her lawyers immediately appealed the ruling, but it would take nineteen months before the courts would retry the case, at which time the decision would be upheld.

Determined to not let her attacker get his wish of keeping her off the courts, Monica began practicing with renewed vigor. Rumors began to surface that she was ready to stage her comeback. But taking time off during the Christmas holidays, Monica felt herself spiraling into a depression. "I had been practicing so much, . . . " she said. "I didn't have time to sit down and say, 'Am I O.K. or not?' Then I had this time |during the holidays| and all these memories started coming back."[21]

It was clear that while she might have recovered physically, she was still hurting emotionally. In February she began to see a sports psychologist to try to work through some of her pain.

The longer she was away from the game, the more people began to wonder if she would ever return. Some of the companies that had endorsed Monica pulled back their support because of her inactivity.

But Monica didn't want to rush her recovery and said, "When I play tennis again, I have to play it for the right reason. I don't want to play to get my No. 1 ranking back. I don't want to play for the attention, or to earn more. I don't even want to play because the world wants to see me do it, even though it's nice to know that the world is interested. I only want to play because I love the game, which is the reason I began to play at age 7 in the first place."[22]

During her time off Monica pursued some other interests besides tennis. She studied French, learned to shoot pool, and started playing her guitar, a Fender Stratocaster.

When she began feeling better, her friend Martina Navratilova came to visit. Navratilova had retired from professional tennis and taken over the presidency of the Women's Tennis Association. She was determined to get Monica back playing professionally and suggested they play an exhibition match. Monica agreed. She knew that at last it was time to return.

Eight hundred twenty days after the stabbing, Monica gulped big mouthfuls of air, trying to calm the butterflies in her stomach. Then she stepped out onto the court. The crowd at the Atlantic City auditorium rose to its feet and thundered applause.

After a nervous double fault, Monica started blasting the ball as if she had never stopped playing. At one point, she made such a good shot that Martina bowed before her. Monica won the match in straight sets. Afterward, Martina was impressed. "If anything," she said, "[Monica's] bigger and better and hitting the ball harder which is hard to imagine."[23] The champ was back!

In the Canadian Open, the first official tournament Monica entered, she outplayed her competition and won easily. "I thought I might choke or get uptight on the big points," Monica said. "It's still quite amazing that I'm actually doing it."[24]

Fans looked forward to the day Monica would once again play her rival, Steffi Graf. In her absence, Steffi had returned to first place. But it was decided that Monica would also retain her number one ranking for her first six matches. This meant that Steffi and Monica were tied for first place. They were also linked by one of the most heinous acts in modern-day sports history. What would happen when they finally played against each other again?

It wouldn't take long to find out. Going into her first Grand Slam event since the stabbing, Monica steamrolled through her competition. Steffi Graf did the same. And on September 19, 1995, the two walked out to center court to compete in the finals. "It is a dream finale that has emerged from a nightmare," the New York Times declared. [25]

In a hard-fought match that left fans hoarse from cheering, Steffi won the first set by the slimmest of margins, then lost 0-6 in the second set. Going into the tiebreaking final set, Steffi pulled out ahead and held on to win. It was clear, however, that in this match there was no loser. Monica had shown she was a winner by coming back, making it to the finals, fighting to the finish. She was a winner for battling her demons and refusing to allow the horrific act of a madman to keep her on the sidelines.

At the end of the match, the two players embraced over the net while applause thundered through the stadium.

"I want to thank you," Seles told the fans. "This is one of the reasons I wanted to come back, to feel the electricity. Thank you . . . all of you."[26]

EIGHT

LYNETTE WOODARD

The Harlem Globetrotters' theme song is "Sweet Georgia Brown," a tune as snappy and upbeat as the basketball team itself. The Globetrotters delight audiences with their unique combination of basketball wizardry, outstanding athleticism, and slapstick humor. Taking a free-throw shot, a Globetrotter might use a trick ball that snaps right back to the shooter, or, when a referee makes a call against a player, a bucket of water might be dumped on top of him! In a regular basketball game, these things would not be allowed, but the Globetrotters are not a regular team.

Founded in 1927, the Globetrotters were originally from Chicago. Their coach, Abe Saperstein, came up with the name Harlem Globetrotters. He picked *Harlem*, the predominantly black neighborhood of New York City, because he wanted the public to know that the team was all black. He picked *Globetrotters* to make people think they traveled all over the world, even though at first they had little money for traveling expenses and only played nearby teams.

The Globetrotters were usually much better than their opponents. No one liked watching one-sided games, so the Globetrotters did tricks to please the crowds. They'd pass the ball through their opponents' legs, shoot with their backs to the basket, tickle an opponent as he went up for a jump shot. Soon they became known for their funny and unique style of basketball.

The Globetrotters became one of the most beloved teams in the country. They lived up to their name, traveling all over the globe, from Hong Kong to Berlin. In 1952 they even played a special game for the pope at the Vatican. A number of famous NBA (National Basketball Association) players started their professional careers playing for the Harlem Globetrotters, including Wilt Chamberlain and Nat "Sweetwater" Clifton.

For almost fifty years the only female to play with the Globetrotters was nine feet tall and weighed more than 3,000 pounds. She was Bertha, a basketball-shooting elephant. But then, in 1985, Lynette Woodard joined the team. An outstanding basketball player with tremendous grace, speed, and power, she won the hearts of fans and the respect of her teammates.

She said, "I don't know about being a role model, but if I am, then the only thing I can tell people—girls, blacks, anyone—is that everyone has something special about them. Sometimes it's real obvious, sometimes it's not. But if they will cultivate that—with the right reasons in mind—because it comes from within you and not just because someone is praising you, then you've got a chance to do something special, or be something special."[1]

Born in Wichita, Kansas, on August 12, 1959, Lynette's earliest memory was of an air force plane crashing near her family's house. The plane burst into flames, destroying fourteen of their neighbors' homes. For five years the rubble-strewn sites remained vacant, until the city decided to use the land for a basketball court.

It was a dream come true for little Lynette. She loved basketball but had nowhere to practice. Her cousin "Geese" Ausbie had introduced her to the magic of the game. Geese played for the Harlem Globetrotters, and when he would visit, he would entertain Lynette with his awesome ball-handling skills. "It was unreal," Lynette recalled. "I couldn't believe the magnificent things he was doing with a basketball."[2]

Geese taught his eager little cousin how to do tricks, like rolling the ball up her arm, across her shoulders, and down her other arm. "And I kind of tore up the house doing it," Lynette laughed. "Well, not the whole house, but the lamp, the iron, the ashtray, the window in my room."[3]

On the new neighborhood basketball courts, Lynette would practice dribbling, rebounding, shooting. She would bounce the ball off the walls to refine her passing skills and spend hours at the free-throw line making foul shots.

She soon became one of the best players in the neighborhood. "Guys were picking me before they picked their friends," she recalled. "Or I would be doing the picking."[4]

In the tenth grade Lynette easily made the high school's varsity squad. It was "a pretty poor excuse for a team," Lynette said.[5] The coach had trouble getting good teams in the league to play against. But Lynette almost single-handedly turned the basketball program around. During her three years at Wichita North, she led the team to three city championships and two state championships. In one game, she scored fifty points!

Lynette proudly said, "When I first started playing for North, no one really attended the games. Now you have as many people at the girls' games, as you have at the boys'."[6] Lynette helped people realize that watching girls' basketball games could be just as exciting as watching boys' games.

By Lynette's senior year, she had earned a reputation as one of the top players in the nation. She received numerous letters from colleges offering her scholarships to play for their teams. After much deliberation, she decided to play for Kansas University.

Coach Marian Washington's style appealed to Lynette. "Coach Washington said to me," Lynette recalled, " 'I can teach you, I can groom you.' I knew I was better than anyone in Wichita—of course, I played 24 hours a day! But . . . I had to learn more about the game."[7]

Coach Washington knew she had a special player on her team but treated Lynette like everyone else. She kept pushing Lynette to get better and better, to finesse her game. "There's so much untapped ability [in Lynette]," she said. "It's frightening."[8]

Fans loved watching Lynette. On defense, she was so fast that she would snatch the ball away from the other team, drive the length of the court, fake around a defensive player, and leap to the basket. Sometimes she would seem to hang in midair, defying gravity. Her teammates nicknamed her "Leapin' Lizard." On offense, no one could stop her. She'd grab the ball, shoot it up, and—swish!—another basket.

Lynette was invited to join the nation's top players on the United States National Women's Basketball team. She traveled all over the world, playing against top teams in such countries as Japan, China, and the Soviet Union. In 1980 she made the Olympic team but was disappointed to find that she would not be able to compete because the United States boycotted the games being held in Moscow.

At the end of her senior year at Kansas University, Lynette was awarded the coveted Wade Trophy, given each year to the nation's top female basketball player. She had averaged 26.3 points a game and had scored 3,649 points during her college career—a new national record. She had broken 24 of her school's 32 women's basketball records, was a four-time All-

American, and a two-time Academic All-American, an award given for earning high grades.

Any male college basketball player who had won this much recognition could expect be a top-round draft pick in the NBA. But there was no comparable women's pro league in the United States.

Lynette knew that in Europe there were a number of professional company-sponsored women's teams. Since she could not imagine giving up basketball, she decided to move away from Kansas for the first time in her life. In 1981 Lynette packed her sneakers and basketball and flew to the tiny town of Schio, Italy.

No one on her team spoke English, and at first Lynette was so lonely and scared she spent most of her time crying. But then, "one day in my apartment . . . I was standing in front of the mirror and . . . I looked at myself and said, 'What are you doing? This is crazy.' And I never cried again."[9] After that Lynette led the league in scoring, averaging thirty-two points per game, and won a loyal following of Italian fans. By the end of the season, she felt she had become a stronger person, but she also knew she was ready to return to America.

There still was no professional women's league, so Lynette set her sights on playing for the 1984 Olympic team. To support herself, she decided to take a job as an academic adviser at Kansas University (KU) and volunteered as the assistant basketball coach. Since she was no longer playing on a team, she knew she would have to work hard to stay in shape for the Olympics. When the KU team members ran wind sprints, Lynette would join them. When they jogged laps, she was running, too. Every evening after practice, she would work out in the deserted gym.

During this busy time, Lynette also managed to make a serious commitment to help underprivileged children. She founded a Big Brother-Big Sister program on the KU campus and worked for the Superkids program for the American Lung

Association. In 1982 the NAACP (National Association for the Advancement of Colored People) honored her as the Woman of the Year for her commitment to public service.

Two years later, at the Olympic team tryouts, Lynette was twenty-six, and the oldest player there. It was soon obvious that despite her age, she could outplay just about everyone. She made the team and was elected co-captain.

The United States coach, Pat Summitt, was a tough drill-master. "[Coach Summitt] wants you 150 percent every day," Lynette said. "You can't be down one day and up another. It's the mental toughness she expects from you."[10] She also wanted Lynette to share the ball, and the spotlight, a bit more. Never before had Lynette played with so many other talented players; they could also make the tough shots. On the Olympic team, she learned to feed her teammates perfect passes, to help them set up to score, to think more strategically. With Lynette at the helm, the United States team easily went on to win the gold medal.

After the Olympics, Lynette was once again without a team. Desperate to keep playing, she decided to call her cousin Geese and ask him if he thought the Globetrotters might add a woman to their roster. Geese assured her that it was impossible.

"When I hung up the phone," Lynette said, "my heart hurt. It was really something I had hoped for more than I realized. It was like . . . 'Lord, if you can't let me play anywhere could you at least take this desire away? Let's have a compromise here.'"[11]

But the desire did not go away.

Soon after, Lynette read an inspirational book that suggested people should pray specifically for what they want, no matter how far-fetched. Always religious, Lynette decided to give it a try. She prayed for God to find a way for her to play for the Harlem Globetrotters.

A few weeks later, the Globetrotters announced they were

holding tryouts. They were looking for their first woman player!

The owner of the team had decided to take this radical step because attendance at the Globetrotter games had been slipping since the mid-1970s. He felt that this was due, in part, to the fact that the level of play in the NBA had increased so dramatically that some superstars were regularly performing feats as astounding as those of the Globetrotters.

Also, the team's comedy routines had not been revamped for years. As he said, they "had become frayed and stale . . . . If we didn't change direction quick, there was a good possibility we'd be out of business in a couple of years."[12] The Globetrotter management hoped that hiring a woman would breathe new life into the team and also bring more fans, especially women and girls, to the games.

The Globetrotter players were not easily convinced, however. Larry "Gator" Rivers, a former Globetrotter star, said, "I was crushed, absolutely crushed when I learned about the idea. We strive to be recognized as a legitimate team, yet there are those who say we're only a bunch of clowns. This seemed like just another gimmick."[13] Many of the other players felt the same way. Still, the management decided to go ahead with its plan.

In July of 1985 Lynette and eighteen other top women players went to the tryouts in North Carolina. They all knew it was the only pro basketball job in the country and they all wanted it. At the tryouts the women played their hearts out. They were elbowing each other for rebounds, sinking outside shots, driving into the lanes, passing behind their backs, dribbling between their legs, leaping for rebounds, wrestling each other for loose balls.

Watching on the sidelines, the Globetrotter president was impressed. "It was no longer a question of can a girl play," he said, "but which one?"[14]

Lynette made the final cut and went with ten other finalists to Burbank, California. In the weeks leading up to these final tryouts, she began training even harder than ever. She would wake at five-thirty every morning, lift weights, run wind sprints, then jog for five miles. Afterward, she would go to the gym and practice, practice, practice.

At the tryouts, the women played not only with each other, but also with men. The owners wanted to see how they worked with male teammates and against male opponents. The women also learned some of the Globetrotters' special passing drills. At first it was hard. They bobbled the ball and knocked into each other. But they kept working. When they finally performed the drills without any mistakes, everyone cheered! For a moment they forgot they were competing against each other and slapped each other's hands, gave each other hugs. They knew they had all worked hard, trained for years, and overcome obstacles to get to this moment—they were the best women basketball players in the country.

On the last day, the management announced that although they were all tremendously talented, only one player would go on to become a Harlem Globetrotter: Lynette Woodard.

Grinning from ear to ear, she told a crowd of journalists, "It's a wonderful feeling. I'm so excited I can't hide it. There's a lot to be learned, and I'm ready to work hard."[15] She knew she would have to refine her skills to make tough tricks look easy. "That's the Globetrotter magic," she explained.[16]

Lynette also was fully aware of the impact she could have on women's sports as the first female Globetrotter. As one reporter said, "It seems that people . . . sometimes need to see women perform on the same court as men before they can finally appreciate just how talented women can be."[17] By playing with and against men, Lynette knew she would have a chance to show America just how well women could play basketball.

A similar event had occurred almost fifteen years earlier.

Female tennis champ Billy Jean King challenged male tennis champion Bobby Riggs to a match dubbed the "Battle of the Sexes." Riggs declared, "Girls should stay in the bedroom and the kitchen because they are inferior in the world of competition."[18] After handing him a piglet (as a symbol of his chauvinism), King went on to beat Riggs in straight sets. After that, attendance at women's tennis matches skyrocketed, and the pay women players received increased substantially.

Lynette hoped that by playing for the Globetrotters she would be able to have the same impact on women's basketball. "I want people to see me play with the Globetrotters and say a woman could also have the ability to play in the NBA,"[19] she said.

In November 1985, a little more than a month after joining the team, Lynette put on her red, white, and blue jersey, number sixteen, and took some deep breaths. Her longtime dream was about to come true. She was going to be a Harlem Globetrotter!

When she ran onto the court for her first U.S. game, the crowd in Spokane, Washington, went wild. People were on their feet, cheering. Lynette had as much fun as the crowd. In a quarter and a half, she missed a couple of layups and had the ball stolen, but she also scored seven points. The coach of the defeated Washington Generals said, "She doesn't get a break from us. On the court, my players don't see a boy or a girl."[20] That's exactly what Lynette wanted.

It took some of her teammates a little longer to get used to this idea. Once, when Lynette was knocked to the ground on a rebound, her teammate Sweet Lou Dunbar loped over and whispered, "Darlin', are you OK?"

"Why you fussin'?" Lynette asked him, jumping up to her feet. "What are you doin'?"[21]

Sweet Lou nodded and ran with her down the court.

After Lynette joined the team, attendance shot up 20 percent, and 90 percent of the Globetrotter games were sellouts.

Fans would hold up homemade signs with Lynette's name on them or her number, sixteen. They would give her standing ovations when she ran onto the court, stomp the floor when she made a basket.

Lynette usually played about a quarter and a half (a little more than fifteen minutes). Fans especially loved it when the team included her in their routines. For example, after Lynette was fouled in one game, Sweet Lou turned to one of the referees and asked, "How many shots?"

"Two," he answered.

Lou turned to the other referee and said, "How many shots?"

"Two," the other referee agreed.

"That's four shots!" Lou shouted as Lynette walked to the free throw line, and the crowd burst into loud laughter.[22]

"Making people laugh is the greatest feeling," Lynette said. "With all the terrible things that go on in the world, it's nice to be able to make people forget them and laugh for a few hours."[23]

But being a Globetrotter was also hard work. The schedule was grueling. The team played 180 games a year, usually 8 games in seven days with one day off a month. When she wasn't playing, Lynette was often giving interviews and signing autographs.

Although at five-foot-eleven Lynette was tall for a woman, she was short compared to the men she played with. Night after night she would be smashed by the big players as they drove for the basket or fought for a rebound. "She's tougher than she looks," one of the Washington Generals said. [24] Still, she was often covered with bruises and was sore and aching after the games.

After two seasons with the Globetrotters, Lynette decided it was time to leave the team. She felt confident she had shown the world how well women could play the game and was ready to move on. She spent the next season playing in the women's professional league in Japan. There she earned almost twice her Globetrotter salary (making about $150,000 a year). When the league banned American players, Lynette moved to the European leagues for a season.

When she returned to America, Lynette felt it was time for other pursuits and became the director of athletic development for the Kansas City, Missouri, schools. This job allowed her to continue to work in athletics and help young people push themselves to be the best they can be. She said, "I tell the kids that everybody has a gift. You let it take you as far as it can."[25]

NINE

❧

KRISTI YAMAGUCHI

A small woman, just five feet tall, in a black-and-gold costume stood alone in the middle of the ice. She was thinking about all the years of training that had brought her to this moment—the 1992 Olympic Games in Albertville, France. The first notes of her music echoed in the hushed arena and she glided confidently across the rink. After she completed her first jump, the audience roared its approval. She skated with athleticism and artistry, great speed but also tremendous grace. One reporter raved, "She landed her jumps so softly it seemed as if she were skating in her slippers."[1]

When it was over, the judges awarded her first place. Kristi Yamaguchi was the best skater in the world. Stepping up to the champion's platform, she accepted her gold medal, becoming the first American woman since Dorothy Hamill in 1976 to win an Olympic figure-skating competition. Afterward, she said, "I've dreamed about this since I was a little girl and I first put on a pair of skates. To think about how far I've come, it's all still sinking in."[2]

❧

Both of Kristi Yamaguchi's parents spent time interned in relocation camps set up by the U.S. government during World War II. After the Japanese bombed Pearl Harbor in Hawaii, fear and hostility toward Japanese Americans led the government to force 120,000 Japanese Americans into these camps and to confiscate their property. Although they underwent numerous hardships in the camps, Kristi's parents never dwelt on the past and harbored little resentment toward their country's government. Kristi's father, Jim, became a dentist and her mother, Carole, became a medical secretary. They raised their three children, Lori, Kristi, and Brett, in Fremont, a town in northern California.

Born on July 12, 1971, Kristi was a tiny baby with clubfeet (her toes turned too far inward). To correct this condition, she had to wear special shoes during the day and a heavy brace at night that made sleeping very difficult. She never let her feet slow her down and before long her toes had straightened out.

One afternoon when Kristi was four years old, she went with her mother to a shopping mall that had an ice rink. Watching the other children whiz across the ice, she begged her mother to let her try. Her mother was worried that her little daughter would hurt herself, but she promised Kristi that when she was old enough to go to school she could learn to skate.

After entering first grade, Kristi reminded her mother of her promise. They went to the mall, and her mother rented her a pair of skates. At first Kristi could barely stand up, her ankles wobbled back and forth, and her feet slipped out from under her. But she clutched at her mother's hand and practiced gliding around the rink. Soon she was laughing uproariously. "I loved it," Kristi recalled. [3]

A year earlier Kristi had watched American figure skater Dorothy Hamill win an Olympic gold medal on television. One day, Kristi vowed, she would be as good a skater as Dorothy. She begged her parents to give her private skating lessons so she could learn to jump and twirl like Dorothy Hamill did.

Knowing how much their daughter loved to skate, her parents agreed. When she was seven years old, Kristi started skating with a woman who would become her longtime coach, Christy Kjarsgaard.

It was obvious to Christy that her young pupil had the natural talent and drive to become a top skater. "Kristi was extremely tiny and her jumps were so small," her coach said, "but I remember the determination on her face when she was out on the ice. She really wanted to do each jump properly."[4] Kristi would wake up each morning long before the sun was up. From five until ten o'clock in the morning she would skate at the mall, and then her mother would drive her to school.

When she was twelve, Kristi decided she also wanted to become a pairs skater. In addition to her morning workouts, she now started training with a partner, a boy named Rudi Galindo, for two hours in the evenings. Their coach, Jim Hulick, helped them learn to perform many difficult and dangerous tricks. Rudi would hoist Kristi over his head and launch her into a "throw jump." Kristi knew if they made one mistake, she would go crashing down onto the ice, but she bravely attempted any new routine.

By 1985 the young pair were good enough to compete with other American pairs skaters in the National Junior Championships. They placed fifth. A year later, they had improved dramatically and awed the judges and audience with their "mirror" skating. They performed tricks side by side, mirroring each other in their flashy red costumes. Finishing first, they were ranked as the top junior team in the nation. They were so good that Kristi and Rudi were invited to represent the United States at the World Junior Championships in Yugoslavia, where they placed fifth overall. Although Kristi was pleased with their performance, she wanted to become number one in the world.

To do so, she knew she had to work very hard, and her training schedule became so intense that she no longer went to school, but continued her education with a private tutor. "I did independent study," she said, "and I knew it was good for my career. But I started to feel isolated."[5] Eventually she decided to return to school part-time. Every free moment she spent practicing, practicing, practicing. This left her with little time for friends, dates, or parties. Also, to stay in shape, she had to be careful about what she ate and regularly had to forgo her favorite food—ice cream. Kristi admitted, "Sometimes I just wanted to let loose and not worry about training, but long-term I was aware of what was important to me in life [skating], and that kept me in line."[6]

All of her diligence paid off. When she was sixteen years old, she took first place in both the singles and pairs categories at the World Junior Championships. Despite this success, Kristi was anxious. She would soon have to start competing against adults. Would she be good enough?

Her first big adult competition was the 1988 U.S. Nationals. Each year the winners of the Nationals go on to compete in the world championships. During Olympic years, the top three medalists at the Nationals are invited to join the U.S. Olympic team. Kristi knew that if she did well she would have a chance to represent the United States at the 1988 Olympics in Calgary, Canada. But she finished a disappointing tenth in singles and fifth in pairs. She vowed to work even harder and try to do better the next year.

That year, however, she discovered that her pairs coach, Jim Hulick, was seriously ill with AIDS. Rudi and Kristi decided that at the 1989 Nationals they would try to skate as perfectly as possible. It would be their tribute to their beloved coach.

The Nationals were being held in Baltimore, Maryland, and as the first strains of the music from *Romeo and Juliet* filled the huge arena, Kristi and Rudi glanced at their coach before beginning their program. When they landed side-by-side triple flips (the only pair in the world to do this trick), the 10,000 fans roared. "This program is simply wonderful," Dick Button, the announcer said, "absolutely thrilling."[7] The young pair were awarded the championship. Coach Jim Hulick beamed with pride.

But Kristi wasn't finished. She still had to skate in the women's singles competition. The skaters were required to perform a short program, a long program, and compulsory figures. Kristi always had the most difficulty with her compulsory figures. For these she was required to trace precisely ordered marks, like figure eights, in the ice. One reporter half-jokingly called them the "painful multiplication tables of sport."[8] At the Nationals, Kristi had trouble with her compulsories and finished in eighth place. After a successful short program, she was in fourth place. Now it was time for her favorite event, the long program.

In the seven minutes she was on the ice, she completed seven perfect triple jumps (spinning around three times in the air). One reporter said, "Yamaguchi performed a breakneck routine that was . . . technically among the most difficult in the world."[9] The crowd rose to their feet, giving her a standing ovation. She had won the long program and came in second place overall. It was the first time in thirty-five years a woman had taken two medals at the Nationals.

These victories earned her a spot on the U.S. pairs and singles skating teams at the 1989 World Championships in Paris, France. At this event, she placed sixth in singles and fifth in pairs.

When she returned home, her school classmates gave her a senior varsity letter jacket to recognize her athletic achievements, even though she hadn't participated on any of their teams. That June she graduated with the rest of her class and soon after, coach Christy announced her plans to get married and move to Edmonton, Canada. Kristi decided to join her and moved away from home.

"It was hard to be apart from my family that first year," Kristi said. "I moved the day after high school graduation, so I missed the parties and that feeling of 'school's out.' . . . One thing that made it easier was that the skaters in Edmonton were really nice and we got to be normal friends outside the rink."[10]

Kristi returned regularly to San Francisco to train with Rudi and coach Jim Hulick for pairs competition. As the year progressed, Kristi began to realize that Jim was dying. "Jim seemed to push his illness aside and focus more on us," Kristi recalled. "I think he sacrificed a lot of his health for our skating."[11] On December 10, 1989, he passed away. Kristi's friend, Tai Babilonia, a former world pairs champion, gave her a heart-shaped earring. "It symbolizes hope and strength and I never take it off," Kristi said.[12]

At the Nationals' Kristi and Rudi once again placed first. In the singles competition, Kristi earned a silver medal despite a surprisingly poor long performance. At the World Championships, Kristi was disappointed when she finished fourth in the singles and fifth in the pairs competition.

She realized that she needed to concentrate on either singles or pairs, but not continue to compete in both. After much soul-searching, she decided to focus on becoming the greatest singles skater she could possibly be. It was a tough decision and Rudi was devastated. But Kristi said, "To improve in one or the other, I had to choose."[13]

She began training with new enthusiasm and lifting weights. "Getting stronger helped her," Kristi's coach said. "It gave her confidence and body control."[14] She also happily quit practicing her compulsory figures when it was announced that they would be eliminated from all major competitions held after July 1990. Without having to practice her figure eights, Kristi could dedicate herself to her jumps, her spins, her graceful moves across the ice.

Coach Christy said, "Kristi has grown up this year. . . . She has matured. You are seeing a different performer out there."[15] This seemed to be true. In three consecutive competitions in 1990, Kristi Yamaguchi took the top prize.

By 1991 she was the clear favorite to win the Nationals. During the competition, however, a blond powerhouse skater from Portland, Oregon, named Tonya Harding, hit a triple axel (a jump in which the skater takes off going forward, turns around three times in the air, and lands backward on the opposite foot). The audience and judges were stunned. Harding was the first American woman ever to make this difficult jump and only the second woman (after Midori Ito of Japan) to ever successfully complete the jump in a competition.

Although Kristi skated with grace and poise in the competition, Tonya was awarded the gold medal. Kristi won the silver. One coach explained, "Jumps are black and white. Tonya makes a triple axel and everybody in the building can see it. It's so much harder to defend your marks on what's tasteful and beautiful."[16]

After that competition, Kristi began practicing the triple axel, but no matter how hard she tried, she couldn't seem to land it. It didn't matter that she could do every other existing jump. It didn't matter that she was arguably the most graceful, accomplished skater on ice. All the media seemed to want to know was why she couldn't do it.

At the World Championships that year, Kristi knew she would be skating against the two women who had landed triple axels—Tonya Harding and Midori Ito. She knew that if both of these women landed their axels, it might be impossible for her to beat them. But on the day of the event, Midori Ito crashed into another skater during warm-ups and was unable to compete. Tonya Harding managed to complete her triple axel during the competition but fell on two other jumps. Kristi fell on a difficult triple salchow (a jump in which the skater takes off going backward, turns three times in the air, and lands backward on the other foot), but impressed the judges with her choreography, her grace, and her finesse. When it was over, she was awarded first place. Harding finished second and their teammate, Nancy Kerrigan, finished third. It was the first time one country had swept the medals in a world competition.

At the 1992 Nationals, Yamaguchi once again won a gold medal, and as the Olympics approached, she was considered one of the top skaters in the world. But the media continued to focus on her inability to complete the triple axel. Carol Heiss, the first woman to ever land a double axel (spinning twice in the air), said, "The jumps were never supposed to mean so much. You need it all: The lightness and the airiness; the music, the personality."[17] Yamaguchi had it all. All except that triple axel.

The press was so obsessed with this one jump, however, that when her coach was asked about it she shot back, "I think [Kristi's] opening combination [a triple lutz jump into a triple toe loop] is the equal of a triple axel in terms of difficulty."[18] Still, the overall assumption remained that if Midori Ito and Tonya Harding were able to hit their triple axels and make no other major mistakes, Kristi would not have a chance to beat them.

Kristi and her parents arrived at the Olympic Village in Albertville, France, in time to join the opening ceremony. During the days right before the competition, Coach Christy said, "[Kristi] skated beautifully . . . Prettier than anything I've seen. A step above. I sat her down and said, 'That's all. You don't have to try to do anything more than what you just did.' It was so beautiful, it didn't matter if a panel of judges put her second. That's what I told her. If you skate like that, it doesn't matter."[19]

During the short program, Kristi watched as Tonya Harding fell attempting her triple axel and Midori Ito fell on a combination of jumps. Kristi, on the other hand, skated flawlessly, putting her in first place. Suddenly it became clear that the gold medal was Kristi's to lose.

In her long program, Kristi skated to the haunting music of *Malagueña*. She nailed her opening combination of jumps, and as one reporter said, she "had the crowd spellbound until more than halfway through, when she fell—the groan!—on a relatively easy triple loop."[20] Suddenly, her gold medal was at risk. She leaped to her feet and continued skating. A jump she'd always had trouble with, the triple salchow, was coming up. Her coach, sitting in the stands, clenched her fists and thought, "She's tired; a smart move would be to play it safe." Kristi's mother thought, "Do a double."[21] Racing across the ice, Kristi leaped into the air and performed a perfect double salchow. As the music ended, she gracefully acknowledged the cheers. Despite her stumble, it had been a beautiful, breathtaking program.

One skating expert said, "The judges . . . loved Yamaguchi's grace and carriage. They loved her speed, her consistency under pressure, the variety of skills displayed within her program. And yes, they loved her artistry. God never gave anyone everything, but Yamaguchi, without the triple axel, is as close to a complete package as women's skating has ever seen."[22]

Standing on the champions' podium, listening to the national anthem, Kristi knew that her dream had come true. She was an Olympic gold medalist, just like her childhood hero, Dorothy Hamill. "I'll never forget the Olympics," Kristi said later. "It's the best experience of my life."[23]

Returning to America, she was a superstar. Within a week her photo appeared on the cover of many popular magazines, including, *Newsweek* and *Sports Illustrated*. In a survey to determine Woman of the Year by the National Coalition of Girls Schools, Kristi finished second, behind First Lady Barbara Bush and ahead of Mother Teresa.

Despite the media attention and publicity, Kristi was able to continue to focus on her skating. A month after becoming an Olympic champion she won her second consecutive World Championship, becoming the first American woman to do so since Peggy Fleming in 1968.

Recognizing Kristi's popularity, companies began bidding for her endorsements, offering her large sums of money to advertise their products. "I was pretty overwhelmed by the number of decisions I immediately had to make after the Olympics," she said. [24] She decided to appear in ads for a cereal, sunglasses, contact lenses, and milk, among others.

Kristi also decided to turn professional and signed the largest show contract in history when she joined the Stars on Ice. "This kind of skating is a lot of fun," Kristi said. [25] She found that, "You can do more with costumes and routines than you can as an amateur. You can get more into the role of the character you're portraying. It's a chance to try different things."[26]

Although she had turned pro, this did not bar her from competing in the 1994 Olympics in Lillehammer, Norway. Deciding whether or not to go to Lillehammer was one of the most difficult decisions of Kristi's career.

"What would it be like to have another Olympic experience?" Kristi asked herself. "It's something I really don't want to pass up. But then again, how much better can it get than Albertville?"[27]

She knew that there would be tremendous pressure on her if she decided to compete. "If it doesn't work out as well for me (in Lillehammer)," she mused, "I'm sure in other people's minds I'd be tarnishing the Albertville experience."[28]

After agonizing months of indecision, Kristi finally announced that she would not go to Lillehammer. "I let my heart decide, and this is what I want to do," she told the press.[29] "I feel relieved. A big weight's been lifted from my shoulders."

She would continue to skate in the Stars on Ice and she hopes that in the future she can go to college and raise a family. For fun, she likes to cheer on the San Francisco Forty-Niners football team, roller-blade, listen to Janet Jackson and Bryan Adams tapes, and "go shopping—anywhere!"[30]

Despite her fame and all the media attention, Kristi has said, "I don't think I've changed . . . I still feel I'm the same old kid, and someone who still wants to be one."[31]

TEN

K IM
Z MESKAL

On Friday, September 13, 1991, gymnast Kim Zmeskal raced across the mat, did three back flips into a back handspring, followed by a flying double-back somersault. As the judges flashed their scores, Kim threw her hands into the air. She had become the first U.S. woman ever to win the World Championship.

"From that moment," her coach said, "she was no longer just a person in the sport of gymnastics. Kim became a personality, an idol for millions of little girls, and an impressive part of U.S. gymnastics history."[1]

Born on February 6, 1976, Kim was the oldest of three children. Both of her parents worked during the day, so Kim stayed at a baby-sitter's house. In the afternoons, she would go to a local gym to watch her baby-sitter's daughter take gymnastics lessons. "I got tired of watching," Kim recalled, "and told them I wanted to start doing it, too."[2]

She was only six years old at the time, but fell instantly in love with the sport. Whenever the coaches asked for a volunteer to try a new trick, Kim's hand was usually the first one to shoot up.

One of the coaches was Bela Karolyi. He had trained the 1976 Olympic gymnastic champion, Nadia Comaneci, in his home country of Romania. Since that time, he had emigrated to the United States and was building his reputation as one of the most successful, demanding, and temperamental gymnastic coaches in America.

At first he wasn't very impressed by little Kim's skills. "She'd fall regularly from the beam during a routine," he said. "She was like popcorn popping on and off."[3] But he also noticed that Kim refused to get discouraged and that she had a fierce competitive spirit.

He decided to invite Kim to join his elite training squad, a group of nine- to ten-year-old gymnasts he was grooming to compete internationally, including, perhaps at the 1992 Olympics. "I called them the Pumpkin generation," Bela said, because they were so young and cute. [4]

In many ways, training to be a top female gymnast is a race against the clock. Young girls and those in their early teens have bodies best suited for this sport. After puberty, girls tend to put on weight and their bodies change and develop in ways that make it more difficult for them to perform the acrobatic routines. Also, the intensity and dedication required to be a top-ranked gymnast is hard to sustain over an extended period of time. Kim knew that for the next few years she would have to put gymnastics at the center of her life if she wanted to have a shot at being the best.

Kim went from taking lessons four times a week to double sessions six days a week. Since she had little time for schoolwork, she took only three classes at Northland Christian School in Houston, Texas. By the time she was in seventh grade, she left school altogether, taking correspondence courses instead so she could increase her training schedule to seven and a half hours a day!

"I don't have a very big social life," Kim admitted. "My training is number one and whatever else doesn't fit in with it, I can't do it."[5] In the little free time she had, Kim liked to watch soap operas or go shopping with her best friend and fellow gymnast, Betty Okino.

Bela was a demanding coach. He wanted his athletes in tip-top form and would put them through grueling strengthening drills. Kim would do hundreds of sit-ups, push-ups, leg-lifts a day. She would do stretching exercises to increase her flexibility. When she mastered the splits, she would put a mat under her feet to force her body to stretch even further, beyond 180 degrees! The rest of her time was spent learning new acrobatic feats and perfecting old ones.

There was so much to learn! Female gymnasts compete in four different events. In the floor exercise a gymnast performs a routine made up of leaps and spins, as well as dance and tumbling moves, on a forty-foot square mat to musical accompaniment. Vaulting requires a gymnast to sprint down a runway, hit a springboard, and perform tricks such as cartwheels, flips, or handsprings over a padded apparatus called a "horse." On the uneven bars a gymnast balances, flips, swings, and flies between two bars set at different heights. The fourth event calls for a gymnast to perform tumbling and balancing tricks on a four-inch-wide balance beam. It is often considered the most difficult event. During competitions, judges award points for each performance; 10.0 points is a perfect score.

Bela knew that the slightest mistake could be the difference between a winning and losing score. With an eagle eye, he would watch Kim practice. If she made the slightest error, he'd bellow, "No! No! No!" and make her go back and start over again. Perfection—it was what he wanted from Kim and from all of his other elite gymnasts. Nothing less was acceptable.

Part of being perfect meant that Kim had to watch her diet. Only four- foot-seven and weighing eighty pounds, she never ate junk food and frequently went to bed feeling hungry. Fortunately, Kim never acquired an eating disorder, a problem that has plagued some gymnasts who feel overwhelmed by the pressure to stay small and thin.

Kim was thirteen when she won her first big meet, the Junior National Championship. This meant she was the best girl gymnast in the United States between the ages of ten and fourteen. She especially captivated the judges and won the hearts of fans with her brilliant floor routine. Smiling at the audience, she was perky and fun to watch.

Kim's idol, 1984 Olympic gold medalist Mary Lou Retton, said, "Everywhere else [Kim's] all business, but [during her floor routines] she looks like she's having a good time."[6]

The next year, Kim competed for the first time against top athletes from around the world at the 1990 America Cup. This is one of the most prestigious competitions in the United States, an event Mary Lou won three years in a row. Young Kim startled everyone by winning the championship. Bela said later, "That child dazzled everybody, I mean everyone! Kim . . . became the leading gymnast in America. She was fantastic."[7]

After the America Cup, Kim began preparing for another important meet, the U.S. Senior Nationals. She would be competing against the best gymnasts in the country for a spot on the U.S. National Team. These team members would represent the United States in the world championship competition.

Kim's practices became even more grueling. "You know your own capabilities," Bela said to her, "and I expect you to perform at your highest level."[8]

Some days Kim would feel too sore to climb out of bed, but she'd force herself to pull on her sweatpants and go back to the gym for more practice.

By the time she entered the Nationals, Kim had performed her routines so many times that she could almost do them with her eyes closed. Still, she had to focus on trying to quiet her nerves. After the first two events, she was in second place, trailing the defending U.S. champion, Brandy Johnson, by only 0.05 point.

While Kim was waiting for her next event, the vault, one of her friends rushed over and told her that Brandy had fallen off the balance beam. Kim had a chance to take over the lead. She clenched her fists and started sprinting down the runway. Her vault was almost flawless. The judges awarded Kim a near-perfect score of 9.975. She had taken over first place and would go on to win the meet. Kim Zmeskal was the number one gymnast in the country.

After the Nationals, Kim was invited to compete in the 1990 Goodwill Games in Seattle, Washington. This meet takes place every four years and was originally established to foster better relations between the United States and the former Soviet Union.

The Soviet teams were always a powerful force in gymnastics, and the U.S. teams had never before beaten them in the Goodwill Games. But Bela was optimistic. "You can expect a big surprise," he said. "Because these kids are gonna carry with them not just a hunger of the big performance but a pride of competing in this country, and the public is going to carry them on their wings."[9]

The night before the competition, Kim was worried. She was having severe pain in her left wrist and heel. Every time she moved her hand, a stabbing sensation would rush up her arm. But Kim told the trainers she would compete despite the pain.

The first day of the games was the team competition and the United States drew the balance beam as the opening event. Bela was dismayed. "That is like a ditch, a hell," he declared dramatically. [10] He knew that nervous energy at the start of the meet can translate into disaster on the narrow balance beam. To have a chance of upsetting the Soviets, the U.S. team members knew they had to stay calm and focused.

Ignoring her sore wrist, Kim performed expertly on the narrow balance beam. She was steady and confident. After she dismounted, the huge crowd thundered applause and the judges flashed a high 9.90.

When the day's events were over, Kim had scored the most points of any gymnast, and the U.S. had lost by only 0.275 point. "This was the best performance we've ever had against the Soviets," Bela exclaimed.[11]

The next day was the individual competition, and although Kim had led the day before, everyone started with a clean slate. On her first event, the uneven bars, Kim at one point spun around but let go of the bars too early. Although she did quite well in the other events, she finished the meet in a disappointing sixth place. Kim knew she could do better and was anxious to meet the Soviets again.

She wouldn't have long to wait. At the United States versus the U.S.S.R. meet at San Jose State University a few weeks later, Kim won the individual championship. It was a satisfying end to the 1990 season. Kim had become the number-one woman gymnast in the nation and proved that she could hold her own against the best gymnasts in the world. She had won five major tournaments and was awarded the 1990 Female Athlete of the Year in gymnastics by both the United States Olympic Committee and the United States Gymnastics Federation. Kim was suddenly inundated with interview requests from journalists around the country, and wherever she went people asked her for her autograph.

Unfortunately, Kim had a disappointing meet in Barcelona, Spain, the location for the upcoming 1992 Olympics, and she did poorly at the 1991 America Cup. She was still suffering from wrist pain and perhaps did not put forth her best effort. Bela growled that gymnasts may "have a tendency to relax, to say, 'Well, I'm pretty good . . . . I'm super good, and I'm taking it a little bit easier.' This happened to Kim pretty evidently."[12]

His comments fired up Kim's competitive spirit and in her next match, the International Mixed Pairs Competition on February 26, 1991, she won the championship. She then went on to once again win the National Championship. In August she flew to Indianapolis for what would become the most important meet of her career, the World Championship. Next to the Olympics, the World Championship is the most prestigious event in the sport of gymnastics. Top athletes from a record-setting fifty-two nations would be competing. Kim was thrilled that in 1992 the event was being held in her own country and hoped she would be able to help the U.S. team win its first medal in this competition.

Journalists could not resist comparing the United States' star, Kim, to the Russians' premiere gymnast, defending world champion and 1988 Olympic gold medalist Svetlana Boginskaya. One reporter commented, "The first names begin to tell the story. Kim versus Svetlana. Short, compact, snappy versus long, graceful, svelte."[13] Kim tried to ignore the media hype and focus only on what she could control—her own performance.

The meet began with the compulsories, a set of prescribed routines the gymnasts had to complete in each event. After all the scores were compiled, the United States was in second place, ahead of the powerful Romanians but behind Russia.

Svetlana helped pull the Russians farther and farther ahead. Meanwhile the Romanians were snapping at the heels of the young American team, until they were tied with only one event left, the vault. "When they tied us, it made us a little nervous," Kim admitted. [14]

She was the last competitor. She would be allowed two vaults and the highest score would count. On her first vault,

Kim scored a 9.962. It was good enough to ensure that the United States had won the silver medal.

But Kim wasn't ready to celebrate yet; she still had one more vault. Bela told her she could do even better. Kim nodded. She raced down the runway, hit the springboard, and did a round-off cartwheel into a backflip. When she landed, it was as if she had glue on her feet—not a single wobble. The crowd went wild. Spectators knew they had witnessed something rare—perfection. The judges flashed her score, a 10.0. Bela enveloped Kim in a bearhug.

The individual competition was two nights later. Kim's parents had come to Indianapolis to cheer her on and were almost as nervous as Kim. "You'd like to be out there helping her," Kim's dad said, "but you know you can't. You have to sit back as a parent and watch from the stands."[15]

As the competition began, it was clear that Kim and Svetlana were the gymnasts to watch. In the first event, Kim performed a near-replica of her perfect vault and shot into first place. In response, Svetlana performed an almost flawless beam routine and was a close second. They continued neck and neck throughout the meet, both gymnasts performing near-perfect routines. Going into the last event, Kim was ahead by a narrow 0.037 point.

Walking to the mat for her floor exercise, Kim was absolutely focused. She knew she had to give the best performance of her career. She burst across the floor, tumbled beautifully, held her landings, grinned up at the stands. The audience was on its feet. Four of the six judges flashed a perfect 10. It was all over. Kim Zmeskal was the new world champion!

She was an instant media celebrity and became the first gymnast to be elected Sportswoman of the Year by the United States Olympic Committee. She was also elected the March of Dimes Female Athlete of the Year, and ABC *Wide World of Sports* Woman of the Year.

Kim had one goal left: to make the 1992 U.S. Olympic team and win a medal in Barcelona, Spain. As the world champion, she was a favorite. She further solidified her reputation by winning the 1992 America Cup and the U.S. Senior Nationals. By the time she made the Olympic team, Kim seemed to be almost invincible. But beneath her perky smile, Kim was in excruciating pain. She had seriously hurt her left leg during a practice session and continued to suffer from a stress fracture in her left wrist.

Still, she bravely refused to acknowledge her problems to the reporters who were heaping pressure on her, declaring her the athlete to defeat. After years of intensive training, Kim refused to let injuries keep her from realizing her dream of competing in the Olympics.

The first day of competition was the team compulsories. Kim's teammates got off to a solid start and when it was her turn, she stepped up to the balance beam with her wrist and ankle heavily bandaged. She took a deep breath and began performing the required skills, one after the other, with confidence and grace. Preparing for the designated tumbling run—a cartwheel into a back handspring into a jump—she looked down the length of the beam, the way she had done thousands of time in practice. She did a perfect cartwheel, but as she flew backward into the handspring, her body veered ever so slightly to the side. She was off-balance. Kim flailed her arms in the air, desperately trying to realign herself, but she could not stop from tumbling to the ground. Jumping back up, she kept thinking, "I didn't fall."[16] She finished with a dazed look on her face.

Her poor score would not count because each team's lowest score was thrown out. Still, Kim was furious with herself. She knew she had not lived up to her own abilities. She vowed to do better and performed solidly in every other compulsory event. The next day, in the team optionals, Kim outscored every other athlete and helped lead the United

States to a bronze medal victory. Standing on the award podium, Kim knew her dream had been realized. She was an Olympic medalist.

But she was not satisfied with third place. She set her sights on winning a gold in the individual competition. She would begin with her favorite event, the floor routine. In practice the day before, the pain in her wrist had grown worse. The wrist would no longer withstand the pressure of her toughest tumbling moves. Kim had to face the truth. She would have to cut some of the most difficult moves out of her routine. It was a terrible disappointment. She had worked so hard to master these feats and now her body would not let her perform them.

No one watching her floor routine would have guessed the frustration and pain Kim was feeling. She jumped and spun across the mat, flew through the air, dazzled the crowd. Bela was beaming as she went into her last tumbling run. And then, she bounced out of bounds. It was a mistake costly enough to knock her out of medal contention. Her dream for a gold was shattered.

Although devastated, Kim performed well in the rest of the events, including a superb routine on the bars, and placed tenth overall. Her teammate, Shannon Miller, managed to win a silver medal.

Kim was a good loser. "I'm happy the team won a bronze," she said. "And I'm happy and proud for Shannon."[17] In the event finals, it seemed as though Kim's spirit had finally been broken. She placed last on the vault and sixth on the floor exercise. It was a disappointing finish to a disappointing Olympics. Still, as one observer stated, "Although Zmeskal failed to meet expectations of others, she obviously didn't let herself down. During the past few years she has won with humility, and at Barcelona she lost with grace. She proved her worth as a champion and exemplified the Olympic creed, which begins with, 'The important thing in the Olympic Games is not to win, but to take part.'"[18]

When Kim returned to her home in Houston after the Olympics, the airport was filled with cheering supporters. Kim realized for the first time how much her fans loved her. "I've learned you don't have to win first place to win," she said. "People have been so supportive. . . . This hasn't been bad for me at all, not winning a gold medal. It's almost better."[19]

Kim returned to school full-time, got her driver's license, and started trying to live a more "regular" teenage life. Before long, though, she could not resist going back to the gym. She continues to train and perform in exhibition meets.

Although she made many sacrifices for her sport, Kim never regretted it. She said, "I don't think I'd be as tough or be able to concentrate as well if I hadn't done this. . . . I can't say it's always been fun, but I've had a goal and I've put everything into it."[20]

SOURCE NOTES

ONE: BONNIE BLAIR

1. Tom Wheatley, "Gaining an Edge: Blair, Here for Gala, Calls Festival a Taste of Olympics," *St. Louis Post-Dispatch* (June 19, 1994), F1

2. Laurel Shaper Walters, "Blair Won't Slow Down or Lose Perspective," *Christian Science Monitor* (July 5, 1994), Sports section, 15.

3. Ibid.

4. Judith Graham, ed., *Current Biography Yearbook* (New York: H. W. Wilson, 1992), 71.

5. John M. McGuire, "Champaign on Ice," *St. Louis Post-Dispatch* (April 17, 1994), C1.

6. Dave Kindred, "Proving Her Precious Mettle," *Sporting News* (March 7, 1994), 15.

7. Cathy Breitenbucher, *Bonnie Blair: Golden Streak* (Minneapolis: Lerner Publications, 1994), 25.

8. Graham, *Current Biography Yearbook*, 72.

9. "Goldrush '88," *Life* (February, 1988), 77.

10. Breitenbucher, *Bonnie Blair: Golden Streak*, 30.

11. Merrell Noden, "One-Woman Ice Show," *Sports Illustrated* (January 15, 1990), 92.

12. "Speed Skating: Bonnie Blair," *Newsweek* (February 10, 1992), 59.

13. Brian Cazeneuve, "Skating First," *Sporting News* (February 14, 1994), S15.

14. William Plummer and Joel Stratte-Mcclure, "Bonnie Blurrr " *People* (February 24, 1992), 42.

15. Sally Jenkins, "A Bonnie Blare," *Sports Illustrated* (February 17, 1992), 38.

16. Breitenbucher, *Bonnie Blair: Golden Streak*, 51.

17. Walters,"Blair Won't Slow Down or Lose Perspective," Sports, 15.

18. Philip Hersh, "Bonnie, We Just Met Ye," *Chicago Tribune* (February 17, 1995), 1.

19. Walters, "Blair Won't Slow Down or Lose Perspective," Sports, 15.

20. "Blair Wins 500m Speedskating," *Associated Press News Service* (February 19, 1994, CD Newsbank Comprehensive)

21. Walters, "Blair Won't Slow Down or Lose Perspective," Sports, 15.

22. Wheatley, "Gaining an Edge," F1.

23. Diane Pucin, "Bonnie Blair Says She's Retiring on her Own Terms," *The Philadelphia Inquirer* (February 18, 1995), CD Newsbank Comprehensive

TWO: FLORENCE GIFFITH JOYNER

1. Megan Othersen, "Going With the Flo," *Runner's World* (May, 1992), 56.

2. Pete Axthelm, with Pamela Abramson, "A Star Blazes in the Fast Lane," *Newsweek* (September 19, 1988), 55.

3. Ibid., 56.

4. Stephanie Mansfield, "Go With the Flo," *Vogue* (April, 1989), 404.

5. Kenny Moore, "Very Fancy, Very Fast," *Sporting News* (September 14, 1988), 160.

6. Axthelm, "A Star Blazes in the Fast Lane," 56.

7. Moore, "Very Fancy, Very Fast," 160.

8. Ibid.

9. Craig A. Masback, "Siren of Speed," Ms.(October, 1988), 35.

10. Kenny Moore, "Special Fire," *Sports Illustrated* (October 10, 1988), 48.

11. Masback, "Siren of Speed," 35.

12. Susan Reed, "Flashy Florence Griffith Joyner will be the One to Watch-and Clock-in the Women's Sprints," *People* (August 29, 1988), 60.

13. Ibid.

14. Moore, "Very Fancy, Very Fast," 161.

15. Kenny Moore, "Get Up and Go," *Sports Illustrated* (July 25, 1988), 17.

16. Ibid.

17. Elle McGrath, "For Speed and Style, Flo With the Go," *Time* (September 19, 1988), 52.

18. Reed, "Flashy Florence," 61.

19. Ambry Burfoot, "Flash Prance," *Runner's World* (December 1988), 48.

20. Moore, "Special Fire," 46.

21. Ibid.

22. Ibid., 48.

23. "No Mo Flo Jo," *Runner's World* (June 1989), 14.

24. Ibid.

25. Charles Moritz, ed., *Current Biography Yearbook* (New York: H. W. Wilson, 1989), 223.

26. Kenny Moore, "The Spoils of Victory," *Sports Illustrated* (April 10, 1989), 53.

27. Othersen, "Going With the Flo," 54.

28. Ibid., 56.

THREE: JULIE KRONE

1. Julie Krone, with Nancy Ann Richardson, *Riding for My Life* (Boston: Little, Brown and Company, 1995), 177.

2. Dorothy Callahan, *Julie Krone: A Winning Jockey* (Minneapolis,: Dillon Press, 1990), 61.

3. Krone, *Riding for My Life*, 11.

4. Ibid., 39.

5. William Plummer and Bryan Alexander, "After the Fall," *People* (December 6, 1993), 132.

6. Krone, *Riding for My Life*, 75.

7. Martha Brant, "Back in the Saddle Again," *Newsweek* (June 6, 1994), 84.

8. Krone,*Riding for My Life*, 65.

9. Ibid., 71.

10. Ibid., 74.

11. Martha Weinman Lear, "She's No Jockette," *New York Times Magazine* (July 25, 1993), 22.

12. Mark McDonald, "Back with a Passion," *The Dallas Morning News* (May 29, 1994), B28.

13. Callahan, *Julie Krone: A Winning Jockey*, 37.

14. Krone, *Riding for My Life*, 84.

15. Gina Maranto, "A Woman of Substance," *Sports Illustrated* (August 24, 1987), 64.

16. McDonald, "Back with a Passion," B28.

17. Lear, "She's No Jockette," 21.

18. Krone, *Riding for My Life*, 99.

19. J. E. Vader, "Riding High," *Ms.* (June, 1988), 30.

20. Lear, "She's No Jockette," 38.

21. Krone, *Riding for My Life*, 170.

22. William Nack, "Bittersweet Victory," *Sports Illustrated* (June 14, 1993), 34.

23. Ibid., 35.

24. William Nack, "The Ride of her Life," *Sports Illustrated* (June 13, 1994), 34.

25. Plummer, "After the Fall," 132.

26. Ibid.

27. Nack, "The Ride of her Life," 36.

28. Michael Mayo, "Krone Set Back by Another Spill," *Sun-Sentinel* (January 14, 1995), C1.

29. Ibid.

30. Krone, *Riding for My Life*, 212.

FOUR: NANCY LOPEZ

1. Nancy Lopez, with Peter Schwed, *The Education of a Woman Golfer* (New York: Simon and Schuster, 1979), 150.

2. Ibid., 10.

3. James and Lynn Hahn, *Nancy Lopez: Golfing Pioneer* (St. Paul: EMC Corporation, 1979), 10.

4. Ibid., 13.

5. Lopez, *The Education of a Woman Golfer*, 46.

6. Hahn, *Nancy Lopez: Golfing Pioneer*, 15.

7. Ibid., 23.

8. Lopez, *The Education of a Woman Golfer*, 19.

9. Ibid., 134.

10. John Goldstein, "When All the Elements Come Together, a Player Can Catch Fire and Burn Through the Tour," *Golf* (February 1987), F12.

11. Lopez, *The Education of a Woman Golfer*, 138.

12. Ibid., 140.

13. Frank Defford, "Hello Again to a Grand Group," *Sports Illustrated* (August 5, 1985), 65.

14. John Papanek, "Out of the Swing of Things," *Sports Illustrated* (June 9, 1980), 21.

15. Ibid.

16. "Minus 30 Pounds and a Husband, Golfer Nancy Lopez Carries a Lighter Bag," *People* (June 14, 1982), 88.

17. Ibid., 86.

18. Bruce Newman, "The Very Model of a Modern Marriage," *Golf* (August 4, 1986), 38.

19. David Barrett, "Lopez' Clean Sweep," *Golf* (February, 1986), 72.

20. Ibid.

21. Defford,"Hello Again to a Grand Group," 66.

22. Kevin Sherrington, "Critics Say LPGA Hall of Fame's Entry Requirements Too Strict," *Dallas Morning News* (May 26, 1994), B1.

23. "Victory Qualifies Lopez for Honor," *Nuestro* (February 8, 1987), 7.

24. George White, "Lopez at Home with Kids or Clubs," *Orlando Sentinel* (June 10, 1993), D1.

25. Jim Beseda, "Tug of Family Pulls Lopez Away from Life on Pro Golf Tour," *The Oregonian* (September 5, 1993), B4.

26. Glenn Sheeley, "Atlanta Women's Championship," *The Atlanta Journal* (April 15, 1994),. E5.

FIVE: DIANA NYAD

1. Diana Nyad, *Other Shores* (New York: Random House, 1978), 152.

2. Emily Greenspan, "Out of the Water and Onto the Airwaves," *Ms.* (March 1985), 74.

3. Ibid., 76.

4. Nyad, *Other Shores*, 71.

5. Janice Kaplan, "Marathon Woman," *Seventeen* (February 1976), 149.

6. Nyad, *Other Shores*, 37.

7. Dan Levin, "A Dunk for the Apple," *Sports Illustrated* (October 20, 1975), 89.

8. Kaplan, "Marathon Woman," 149.

9. Levin,"A Dunk for the Apple," 89.

10. Nyad, *Other Shores*, author's note.

11. Ibid., 138.

12. Greenspan, "Out of the Water and Onto the Airwaves," 76.

13. Nyad, *Other Shores*, 103.

14. Jane Shapiro, "Diana Nyad: The Obsession of the Long-Distance Swimmer," Ms. (August, 1978), 29.

15. Dan Levin, "An Ill Wind that Blew No Good," *Sports Illustrated* (August 28, 1978) 23.

16. Ibid.

17. Greenspan, "Out of the Water and Onto the Airwaves," 77.

18. Donna Foote, "And One Who Failed," Newsweek (August 28, 1978), 59.

19. R. Dean Straw, "The World's Longest (Electronics-Assisted) Swim," *Motorboating and Sailing* (January 1980), 171.

20. Greenspan, "Out of the Water and Onto the Airwaves," 77.

21. Ibid., 78.

SIX: JOAN BENOIT SAMUELSON

1. Joan Samuelson, "To Dream, to Dare, to Create," *Runner's World* (July 1991), 48.

2. Kenny Moore and Lisa Twyman, "The Marathon's Maine Woman," *Sports Illustrated* (May 2, 1983), 55.

3. Joan Benoit, with Sally Baker, *Running Tide* (New York: Alfred A. Knopf, 1987), 57.

4. Ibid., 59.

5. Samuelson, "To Dream, to Dare, to Create," 47-48.

6. Benoit, *Running Tide*, 83.

7. Moore, "The Marathon's Maine Woman," 58.

8. Benoit, *Running Tide*, 106.

9. Ibid., 110.

10. Moore, "The Marathon's Maine Woman," 58.

11. Benoit, *Running Tide*, 113.

12. Ibid., 156.

13. Ibid., 167.

14. Amby Burfoot, "Cloudy Skies," *Runner's World* (February 1992), 42.

15. Benoit, *Running Tide*, 181.

16. Burfoot, "Cloudy Skies," 42.

17. Benoit, *Running Tide*, 187.

18. Ibid., 192.

19. Ibid., 198.

20. K. C. Johnson, "Samuelson Still has Drive: Chicago Race 1st Step in Olympic Bid," *Chicago Tribune* (October 26, 1994),CD Newsbank Comprehensive.

21. Burfoot, "Cloudy Skies," 42.

22. Bill Littlefield, "Marathon Mom," *Yankee* (April, 1994), 134.

23. Julie Hanna, "Oregon Runner Collapses-After Winning Race," *Chicago Tribune* (October 31, 1994), CD Newsbank Comprehensive.

24. Burfoot, "Cloudy Skies," 41.

25. Samuelson, "To Dream, to Dare, to Create," 48.

SEVEN: MONICA SELES

1. Peter Bodo, "The Second Life of Monica Seles," *Tennis* (March 1994), 45.

2. John Heilpern, "The Softer Side of Seles," *Vogue* (June 1992, 166.

3. Sarah Boxer, "Determined, But in No Great Hurry," *Sports Illustrated* (August 22, 1988), 10.

4. Jim Loehr, "Not Until She's Ready," *World Tennis* (June 1989), 22.

5. I Ibid., 24.

6. Ibid.

7. Cindy Shmerler, "Hitting Out In All Directions," *World Tennis* (August 1990), 30.

8. Alexander Wolff, "Grunt, Squeak, Victory," *Sports Illustrated* (June 18, 1990), 19.

9. Judith Graham, ed., *Current Biography Yearbook* 1992 (New York: H. W. Wilson, 1992), 516.

10. Bodo, "The Second Life of Monica Seles," 44.

11. Sally Jenkins, "Truth or Where?" *Sports Illustrated* (July 29, 1991), 34.

12. Heilpern, 210.

13. Felix Bauer, "Man Knifed Seles So Graf Could Be No. 1," *Reuters* (May 1, 1993, CD NewsBank Comprehensive)

14. Ibid.

15. S. L. Price, "The Return," *Sports Illustrated* (July 17, 1995), 24.

16. Monica Seles, "Working My Way Back," *Tennis* (March 1994), 46.

17. Bodo, "The Second Life of Monica Seles," 45.

18. Seles, "Working My Way Back," 46.

19. Johnette Howard, "Home Alone," *Sports Illustrated* (April 10, 1995), 46.

20. Ibid, 46.

21. Price, "The Return," 24-25..

22. Bodo, "The Second Life of Monica Seles," 42.

23. Harvey Araton, "It Sounds As if Seles is Back," *New York Times* (July 30, 1995), Section 8, 1.

24. Robin Finn, "Seles Appears Invincible in Steamrolling Sabatini," *New York Times* (August 20, 1995), Section 8, 1.

25. Robin Finn, "Seles and Graf Will Keep Their Date with Destiny," *New York Times* (September 9, 1995), Section 1, 27.

26. Steve Wulf, "A Very Happy Return," *Time* (September 18, 1995), 100.

EIGHT: LYNETTE WOODARD

1. Ira Berkow, "Woodard Adds a Special Spirit to Globetrotters," *The New York Times* (February 16, 1986), V9.

2. Franz Lidz, "Is This Georgia Brown?," *Sports Illustrated* (January 6, 1986), 46.

3. Berkow,"Woodard Adds a Special Spirit to Globetrotters," 9.

4. Roy S. Johnson, "Far Above the Crowd," *Sports Illustrated* (January 26, 1981), 41.

5. Ibid.

6. Mathew Newman, *Lynette Woodard* (Mankato, Minnesota: Crestwood House, 1986), 12.

7. Michelle Kort, "Lynette Woodard," *Ms.* (January, 1986), 45.

8. Johnson, "Far Above the Crowd," 41.

9. Berkow, "Woodard Adds a Special Spirit to Globetrotters," 9.

10. Malcolm Moran, "Lynette Woodard Now a Role Player," *New York Times* (July 27, 1984), I4.

11. Kort,"Lynette Woodard," 99.

12. Lidz, "Is This Georgia Brown?," 45.

13. Ibid., 46.

14. Ibid.

15. Bert Rosenthal, *Lynette Woodard: The First Female Globetrotter* (Chicago: Children's Press, 1986), 27.

16. Lidz, "Is This Georgia Brown?," 47.

17. Kort, "Lynette Woodard," 44.

18. Linda Robertson, "Old Obstacles Litter Women's Path to Spotlight," *St. Louis Post-Dispatch* (June 23, 1993), D1.

19. George Vecsey, "The Newest Globetrotter," *The New York Times* (October 13, 1985), V1.

20. Lidz, "Is This Georgia Brown?," 47.

21. Ibid.

22. Berkow, "Woodard Adds a Special Spirit to Globetrotters," 9.

23. Rosenthal, *Lynette Woodard: The First Female Globetrotter*, 41.

24. Berkow, "Woodard Adds a Special Spirit to Globetrotters," 9.

25. "She Showed She Could Play with the Big Guys," *People* (March 7, 1994), 181.

NINE: KRISTI YAMAGUCHI

1. E. M. Swift, "Stirring," *Sports Illustrated* (March 2, 1992), 21.

2. Judith Graham, Editor, *Current Biography Yearbook 1992* (New York: H. W. Wilson, 1992), 619.

3. Shiobhan Donohue, *Kristi Yamaguchi: Artist on Ice* (Minneapolis: Lerner Publications, 1994), 13.

4. Jeff Savage, *Kristi Yamaguchi: Pure Gold* (New York: Macmillan, 1993), 19.

5. Karen Bressler, "Kristi Tells All," *Seventeen* (December 1992), 84.

6. Ibid., 86.

7. Donohue, *Kristi Yamaguchi: Artist on Ice* 29.

8. Frank Defford, "The Jewel of the Winter Games," *Newsweek* (February 10, 1992), 47.

9. Graham, *Current Biography Yearbook 1992* 617.

10. Bressler,"Kristi Tells All," 86.

11. Donohue, *Kristi Yamaguchi: Artist on Ice* 38.

12. Ibid.

13. Graham, *Current Biography Yearbook 1992* 618.

14. Swift, "Stirring," 19.

15. Savage, *Kristi Yamaguchi: Pure Gold* 45.

16. Defford, "The Jewel of the Winter Games," 47.

17. Ibid., 51.

18. Graham, *Current Biography Yearbook 1992* 619.

19. Swift, "Stirring," 20.

20. Ibid., 21.

21. Defford, "The Jewel of the Winter Games," 51.

22. Swift, "Stirring," 21.

23. Donohue, *Kristi Yamaguchi: Artist on Ice* 56.

24. E.M. Swift, "All that Glitters," *Sports Illustrated* (December 14, 1992), 75.

25. Norm Frauenheim, "Olympic Champ Leads Parade," *The Arizona Republic* (January 1, 1993), p. A10.

26. Norm Frauenheim, "Yamaguchi Enjoying Pressure-Free Ice Skating," *The Arizona Republic* (January 6, 1994), D1.

27. Don Banks, "Can it Get any Better Than Gold?" *St. Petersberg Times* (February 8, 1993), C1.

28. Ibid., C1.

29. Bill Glauber, "Norway Won't be Part of Yamaguchi's Routine," *The Baltimore Sun* (March 24, 1993), D1.

30. Bressler, 8"Kristi Tells All," 6.

31. Swift, "All that Glitters," 75.

TEN: KIM ZMESKAL

1. Bela Karolyi and Nancy Ann Richardson, *Feel No Fear: The Power, Passion, and Politics of a Life in Gymnastics* (New York: Hyperion, 1994), 208.

2. Brian Cazeneuve, "Zmeskal Grabs U.S.A.'s First World All-Around Gold," *International Gymnast* (December 1991), 32.

3. Karolyi, *Feel No Fear*, 131.

4. Ibid., 189.

5. "1992 Individual Apparatus World Championships," aired on ABC, April 19, 1992 quoted in Krista Quiner, *Kim Zmeskal: Determination to Win* (East Hanover, New Jersey: The Bradford Book Company, 1995), 102.

6. Mark Starr, "The Little Pumpkin," *Newsweek* (July 27, 1992), 56.

7. Karolyi, *Feel No Fear*, 193.

8. Ibid.

9. Quiner, *Kim Zmeskal: Determination to Win*, 41.

10. Kenny Moore, "Balance of Power," *Sports Illustrated* (August 6, 1990), 22.

11. Ibid., 23.

12. Quiner, *Kim Zmeskal: Determination to Win*, 53.

13. E. M. Swift, "Kim Zmeskal VS Svetlana Boginskaya," *Sports Illustrated* (July 22, 1992), 55.

14. E. M. Swift, "A Wow at the Worlds," *Sports Illustrated* (September 23, 1991), 41.

15. "1991 World Championships: Event Finals," aired on ABC, September 14, 1991, quoted in Quiner,*Kim Zmeskal: Determination to Win*, 89.

16. Tom Weir, "Gritty Zmeskal Regains Footing," U.S.A *Today* (July 29, 1992), E3.

17. "Two 10.0s for women, four More Golds for Scherbo," *International Gymnast* (October 1992), 54 quoted in Quiner, *Kim Zmeskal: Determination to Win*, 161.

18. "Gutsu Is Golden," *International Gymnast* (October 1992), 29.

19. E. M. Swift, "All That Glitters," *Sports Illustrated* (December 14, 1992), 78.

20. Kathryn Casey, "Friends and Rivals," *Seventeen* (June 1992), 87.

FURTHER READING

Aaseng, Nathan. *Florence Griffith Joyner: Dazzling Olympian*. Minneapolis: Lerner, 1989.

Benoit, Joan, with Sally Baker. *Running Tide*. New York: Alfred A. Knopf, 1987.

Breitenbucher, Cathy. *Bonnie Blair: Golden Streak*. Minneapolis: Lerner, 1994.

Donohue, Shiobhan. *Kristi Yamaguchi: Artist on Ice*. Minneapolis: Lerner, 1994.

Karolyi, Bela, and Nancy Ann Richardson. *Feel No Fear: The Power, Passion, and Politics of a Life in Gymnastics*. New York: Hyperion, 1994.

Koral, April. *Florence Griffith Joyner: Track and Field Star*. New York: Franklin Watts, 1992.

Krone, Julie, with Nancy Ann Richardson. *Riding for My Life*. Boston: Little, Brown , 1995.

Lopez, Nancy, with Peter Schwed. *The Education of a Woman Golfer*. New York: Simon and Schuster, 1979.

Newman, Matthew. *Lynette Woodard*. Mankato, Minnesota: Crestwood House, 1986.

Nyad, Diana. *Other Shores*. New York: Random House, 1978.

Quiner, Krista. *Kim Zmeskal: Determination to Win*. East Hanover, New Jersey: Bradford Book Company, 1995.

INDEX